Texas Manners

A Guide to Gracious Living

Cece Neef Brune

Texas Manners

A Guide to Gracious Living

Cece Neef Brune

Republic of Texas Press
Plano, Texas

Library of Congress Cataloging-in-Publication Data

Brune, Cece Neef.
  Texas manners : a guide to gracious living / Cece Neef Brune.
    p. cm.
  Includes index.
  ISBN 1-55622-882-1
  1. Etiquette—Texas. I. Title.

  BJ1859.T4 B78 2001
  395'.09764—dc21   2001031641
                                               CIP

Printed in the United States of America

ISBN 1-55622-882-1
10 9 8 7 6 5 4 3 2 1
0801

All inquiries for volume purchases of this book should be addressed to Wordware
Publishing, Inc., at 2320 Los Rios Boulevard, Plano, Texas 75074. Telephone
inquiries may be made by calling:

(972) 423-0090

Dedication

Texas Manners is dedicated to the ones I love, in alphabetical order, A.J., Dani, and Kimmy.

Contents

Babies

Preschoolers

Contents

The Restless Years

Social Occasions

Out of the Nest

Contents

Debutantes and Escorts

Getting a Job

Miscellaneous

Contents

Dining

Y'all Come Back Now, Ya' Hear?

Alcoholic Beverages

Engagements

Wedding Invitations

Contents

The Wedding

Civic and Charity Events

Government

The Military

Dangerous Territory

Let's Call a Spayed a Spayed

Funeral Etiquette

"If I owned Hell and Texas, I'd rent out Texas and live in Hell."

Philip Sheridan, Union soldier

Preface

What state would have the audacity to have its own etiquette book? Texas, of course! Consisting of 267,277 square miles, it is large enough to contain the states of Delaware, Hawaii, Massachusetts, Maryland, Missouri, New Jersey, New York, Oklahoma, South Carolina, Rhode Island, Vermont, and the District of Columbia, and still have some room left over.

It just figures that with over twenty million citizens, Texas would end up with its share of infamous inhabitants. The Republic of Texas separatists, the cheerleader mom who hired a hit man to eliminate her daughter's rival, and Howard Hughes have all made national headlines. We have a reputation for "big hair," fanatical football fans, beautiful women, big business, and the world's best chicken-fried steak. (Though, I do admit that truly "big hair" is difficult to find these days.) Fortunately, the majority of Texans are friendly, generous, hard-working, and patriotic. We are proud of the many famous musicians, artists, entrepreneurs, and politicians that hail from Texas.

Unfortunately, Texas also has cockroaches, snakes, tornadoes, droughts, dust storms, heat, humidity, and hurricanes. However, we try to maintain a sense of decorum in the face of such adversity. Whether you are a Texan, or just captured by the Lone Star mystique, *Texas Manners* provides a humorous, easy-to-use etiquette reference for the entire family. Not only does it contain standard etiquette practices, but it also includes many subjects never addressed before. Where else could you find out how many kegs of beer you need for a barbecue for 400 people. Know when to wear boots and jeans with a tuxedo jacket. Learn what to do when you come face to fang with a rattlesnake. Discover what you do at a quinceañera.

Acknowledgments

We often use the excuse that we are too busy to sit down to a family meal or write a thank-you note, but we manage to find time to play golf, work out, or go to the movies. My mother, Frances Neef, raised a family of five and still managed to impart the basic social skills to all her children. A sorority sister of mine, Julie Yarbrough, told me when I asked how she managed to maintain her busy schedule, "You always make time for the things that are important to you." I doubt that she even remembers the conversation, but it is as striking a statement now as it was when I was eighteen.

My friends have been exceedingly helpful and supportive of this venture, and I would like to thank the following people who provided research assistance: Terry Atkin, Mary Beck, Anne Billingsley, Grant Billingsley, Randy Brown, Gretchen Davis, Gayle Dodson, Linnie Donnelly, Nina Echterhoff, Susie Evans, Claire Heck, Lavada Helton, Patty Herd, Penny Hudgeons, Lora Jones, Mary Ann Majors, Eileen Piwetz, Helen Shelton, Lois Smitherman, Nina Thomas, Karin Zaya, and especially Vicki Chase. To those who unintentionally helped by writing such quotable notes, please excuse the poetic license used to rephrase or change the names in your correspondence. Thanks to Gina Hickman, Kaye Lane, Melissa Palko, Carolyn Winkler, and the late Frankie Franklin. If it had not been for all the "When is your book going to be finished?" I might not have typed so fast. Thanks to Fran Billingsley, Fern Crume, Paula Douglas, Margie McKinney, Amy Robnett, Betty Thompson, Lissa Wagner, Betty Ward, and the K.I.T. for keeping after me. My petite inspirations were Rachel, Jay, Everett, Christain, Nicole and William Vaughn, and Justin and Grace Vincent. A special thanks goes to Yolanda

Romero for keeping house and home together while I worked on this project.

David Biber and his computer artfully turned my sketches into recognizable objects. Many thanks for a job rapidly and well done. Andy Brinson's creative genius provided the great cover for *Texas Manners*, which I just adore. I would also like to acknowledge the kindness and support I received from Judy Rankin and Tumbleweed Smith.

Who in the world would be lucky enough to have an editor with a delicious sense of humor and a craving for dark chocolate? Not only was she willing to take a chance on a first-time author, but she made the venture into publishing a pleasure for me. A very inadequate but heartfelt "thank you" goes to Ginnie Bivona.

I can't even imagine what my life would have been like without my best friend, Susan Weidner. How do you adequately thank someone for a lifetime of support, commiseration, and silliness?

When inquiring just exactly what I was writing, my husband, A.J., jokingly remarked, "Oh, I see. It's not just etiquette, it's Texas manners." Thanks for the title, Honey, and thirty plus years with you. I am also deeply indebted to my incredible daughters, Kimberly and Danielle, for their enthusiastic editing, constant encouragement, and love. No one could have a more wonderful family. I love them all beyond words.

Cece Neef Brune

Disclaimer

To the best of my knowledge, all the material in *Texas Manners* is accurate and indicative of the generally accepted principles of etiquette. I am not, however, a professional carpet cleaner, dry cleaner, silversmith, doctor, lawyer, or psychologist. Suggestions offered in this book are the current "conventional wisdom." No guarantees or miracle cures should be inferred.

Introduction

My husband, a native Texan, would cringe when I told people that I was born in New York City, so I added the phrase, "but I moved to Massachusetts when I was an infant." He would frown even more. Then I tried, "I was born in the East, but I moved to Texas when I was thirteen." That still wasn't quite what he had in mind. Finally, I came up with "I've lived in Texas most of my life."

As the mother of two daughters, my life was filled with PTA, carpools, and homework. I served as president of many civic organizations, developed a scholarship library for the local high school, and chaired and edited two nonprofit cookbooks. Just when I thought the most difficult part of child raising was over, came the time for dating, college applications, sorority rush, debutante presentations, and job searches. Then, after years of being identified only as "Mom," I found myself the "unemployed" mother of two charming and independent young women.

Relishing the time to spend with my husband and to finally tackle that long list of those "someday I will..." items, I had no intention of finding a new career. I learned how to quilt, started watercolor classes, and began compiling a cookbook. While trying to plan a wedding shower, I started researching shower etiquette. I was frustrated by the lack of information and how poorly organized and indexed etiquette books were. It had been years since I had written anything other than a thank-you note, but soon my days were devoured by research and writing.

My husband blames my preoccupation with etiquette on my early childhood spent in New England, but my daughters claim that it is just that I have always had an answer for every question.

Babies

I happen to love babies. It is no coincidence that babies have the place of honor as the very first chapter in this book. After all, you have to be born before you can learn to be mannerly. I did not, however, put babies first on the agenda as a subtle hint to my daughters that I hope to be a grandmother someday. They have already observed the glassy look of addiction I have whenever I enter a clothing store for infants. I have taken courses in French sewing: all the better to make charming baby frocks. I have two adorable handmade baby quilts and a youth chair for my dining room table. I have never packed up the children's toys to an inaccessible area of the attic. In other words, while I am not *expecting* any babies, I learned from my Girl Scout days to be prepared.

Texas has the fifth highest birth rate in the nation, with an amazing 900 births per day. With a population of twenty million and growing, it is likely that you, or someone you know, will experience an addition to the family.

Baby Showers

Most baby showers are held before the baby is even born, thus eliminating the problem of the infant committing a social faux pas at his/her first outing. Sometimes showers are held after the birth of a child or following an adoption. Either option is acceptable; there is just a little more pressure on the baby to perform at the second.

You may host a baby shower for anyone who is expecting or adopting her/his first child, as long as you are not related to that person. I know you love your sister, but when a relative hosts a shower it becomes a flagrant plea for gifts, no matter how pure your intentions. Let someone who loves your sister just a little bit less than you host the party.

Be sure to check with the expectant mother and verify that she wants to have a shower before you go sailing ahead with your plans. If there are multiple hostesses, all the hostesses must plan to attend the event.

A shower for a second or third child is not proper, but you may have a celebration of another sort to honor the new child. An exception might be if a large gap exists between the last child and the latest one, then a shower would be appropriate.

When the average population was having children in their late teens and early twenties, party games were all the rage at showers. Now that the average age of first-time mothers is increasing, this silliness has been put to rest. Conversation has taken the place of games.

The Invitation

Keeping in mind the mother's taste, select an invitation. Do not list where she has registered. Do include the day, date, time, and your address and phone (for reply) along with the honoree's name.

A sample casual invitation:

You're invited to a
Baby Shower
honoring

Michelle Vaughn

Saturday, August 15th
2 o'clock

at the residence of
Frances Ballard
1303 Stanwick

R.S.V.P.   Casual
682-2211

Shower Gifts

If you are invited to a baby shower, check to see if the mother has registered her selections. You do not have to restrict your purchase to something on the selection list. Unless the mother has specified a need for newborn clothes, six months to one-year size is always appropriate, but consider what season it will be when the baby will be wearing the outfit. If the shower is for twins, take two gifts.

🌱 You do not need to send a gift if you do not attend the shower, but you may send one if you wish.

🌱 Sign your gift card with your first and last name, but do not use any title (Mr., Mrs., Dr.). If using an engraved calling card as an enclosure card, add a message on the back and sign it informally.

🌱 Respond to the invitation within three days by phone or in writing.

The following is an excerpt from a note of regret that I received from the out-of-town grandmother of the honoree:

The baby shower for Vicki will be such an exciting event. I regret that I will be unable to accept your invitation. Best wishes for a perfect day. I will be thinking of all that I am missing.

Baby Shower Thank-You Notes

If the gifts are opened in the presence of the guests and they are thanked personally, you do not have to write a thank-you note. Of course, it would be just fine if you did. A thank-you note is always appreciated. The same is true for gifts brought to the hospital after the baby arrives: If thanks are given in person, you do not need to write a note.

If you write a note after the baby arrives, do not sign it with the baby's name. Only the individual writing the note should sign his/her name, but you may mention other family members in the body of the thank-you note. Use a correspondence card or a fold-over note with black or dark blue ink. Write your return address, with no name, on the back flap of the envelope.

Selecting a Name

I understand that this process has caused many a family argument. Really, it is nobody's business but the parents'. If you love the expectant parents, or even like them a little, stay out of it. Listen to their list of names with an expressionless face and sympathize with how difficult it is to decide between Esmeralda and Hermione. Somehow, we have all managed to grow into our names or have changed them permanently in court.

There are a few suggestions I would make.

🌱 Legal names may consist of a first and last name; first, middle and last name; initials and last name; or first, middle initial, and last name. (See Hyphenated Last Names.)

❧ Names with an unequal number of syllables in the first and last name usually sound better. Beverly Hill sounds better than Bob Hill (who could have started out as Robert Hill, which sounds just fine).

❧ The name should be easy to spell and pronounce.

❧ Make sure the initials do not spell out something you would rather not see on a monogram.

Like: Stephen Oliver Brown

❧ If you want to incorporate a family name, you can always use it as a middle name.

❧ If there are several generations of men with the same name, ponder what name you will use to differentiate him from all the other William Robert Townsends in your family.

William Robert Townsend
Bill Townsend
Big Billy Townsend
Little Billy Townsend
Willy Townsend

Texan and world champion boxer George Foreman solved the problem of naming his sons by naming them all George Foreman: George the first, George the second, etc.

When it comes to names, Texans have a few unique ideas. Female offspring may be named after their father or other male family member. One of my sorority sisters was named Ralph.

Two-name first names are also common, as in Betty Lou and Billy Bob, which are typically pronounced as if there were one word.

A terrifying new trend has emerged in which a few syllables of each of the parents' names are merged to form a new name. For example, Shawn and Monique would name their little bundle of joy Shanique. I would avoid this at all costs, as well as naming your child for the place of his/her conception: Mercury Marquis or Secluded Falls.

Birth Announcements

Well, you pretty much have free reign here, but I would stay away from anything too cute. With the advent of computer generated material, you can produce a lovely announcement at minimal expense. Of course, you may order all kinds of elaborate engraved announcements tied with tiny bows or French wire ribbon. The choice is up to you. The most formal announcement is an engraved calling card for the baby tied to a large card engraved with the parents' names. What little Farquhar would do with his engraved calling cards is beyond me, unless little Farquhar is heir apparent to a throne.

Pink for girls and blue for boys are still the dominant color choices, but gender neutral colors are also fine.

Formal:

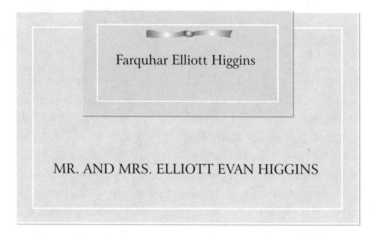

Farquhar Elliott Higgins

MR. AND MRS. ELLIOTT EVAN HIGGINS

An address may be included in the lower right-hand side of the large parent card, and a birth date may be included in the same area on the infant's card.

Informal:

> Carol and Bob Hill
>
> announce the arrival
> of their daughter
>
> Justine Marie
>
> Saturday, May 15th
> 6 lbs. 3 ozs.

Adoptions

Similar style cards may be used for adoption announcements. The infant's or child's age or the word "adoption" may be used in the announcement.

The receipt of a birth announcement does not require a gift.

The Christening

A christening is a religious event in which children are baptized. It may take place during a regular church service or may be a private event. Catholic children are baptized soon after birth and Protestant babies usually within six months. Some religions, such as Baptists, hold baptisms later in life.

Parents may make a donation to the church in the name of their child at the time of baptism. Invite the officiant to any celebration following the christening.

Invitations may be oral or written.

Please join us
at the Christening
of
Justine Marie Crawford

Sunday, May 15th
ten o'clock
Grace Presbyterian Church

and brunch following the ceremony
16 Sutton Avenue

Reply 687-6020

Serving as a Godparent

☙ Godparents attend the christening ceremony and hold the infant during the ceremony.

☙ Godparents promise to be responsible for the child's religious upbringing.

☙ They should give the baby a gift.

☙ They should wear appropriate church clothes, but women should not wear black.

☙ Participants should be invited to attend any celebration following the christening.

Non-Christian Naming Ceremonies

Jewish Ceremonies

Jewish males are circumcised in a ceremony called a Bris, traditionally on the eighth day after they are born. A female child is named on the first Sabbath day after her birth.

Some sort of social event, from a lunch to small party, is often held following the religious ceremony to name a child. If you are invited, you should bring a gift for the baby. A small reception might include cake and champagne to toast the new arrival.

Hindu Ceremonies

Hindu babies are named at a rice eating ceremony when they are about six months old. This celebrates the child's first solid food. These ceremonies usually take place in the home and may be followed by a reception with traditional Indian food and possibly music. Alcohol is not served. A gift for the child is appropriate. If the service takes place in a temple, women should cover their arms and their legs to below the knee.

Islamic Ceremonies

Not all Moslems follow this practice, but an akikah ceremony may be held to welcome a new baby. When attending services at a mosque, women must cover their arms, head, and their legs to below the knee. Shoes should be removed before entering the mosque. A reception may follow, but alcohol will not be served. A cash gift for the baby is appropriate.

Sip and See

You might remember this activity from your wedding. Everyone drops by for tea and looks at all your wedding loot. Now, they come to see the baby: yours, your daughter's, or your daughter-in-law's. The invitation should be simple, outlining the nature of the activity, the time and date, location, and the honoree. The hostess(es) listed on the invitation must attend the party.

I know you want to put "no gifts, please" on the invitation, but do not do it. Putting "no gifts" on any invitation is rude: It implies that just because you are having a party you would *expect* people to bring a gift. If you prefer that guests did not bring gifts, casually circulate the idea to your friends. If some of your guests bring gifts, put them in another room and open them after everyone leaves.

Of course, you will write a lovely handwritten thank-you note on white or ecru correspondence cards (or fold-over notes) and under no circumstances will you sign the baby's name. Unless your infant is a prodigy, you will be writing the letter for him or her.

Sample invitation:

> *You're invited to the Dallas debut*
>
> *of*
>
> *Lissa Ann Vaughn*
>
> *Wednesday, June 1st*
> *at*
> *three o'clock*
>
> *at the home of her grandmother*
>
> *Elsie Hunt*
> *1303 Sharp Street*

Babies are an affirmation that another generation of Texans will follow in our footsteps. They fill us with the hope that they will live better, safer, and kinder lives than those who came before them. They reach for us with open arms and open hearts; a precious gift for parents, grandparents, and great-grandparents.

"The population of some small Texas towns never changes. Every time a baby is born, someone leaves town."

Anonymous

Preschoolers

Somewhere along the road to raising a child, a parent must decide where to draw the line between a child's right to self-expression and what they need to learn to advance to adulthood without being rude and disrespectful. Generations have vacillated between the "spare the rod and spoil the child" philosophy and that of discipline being hazardous to a child's well-being. Teaching your child manners may be the simplest answer to the problem, but it can also be very effective. If children are taught to respect others and follow certain guidelines of society, it can only be to their advantage. Ultimately, we are judged by the way we interact with others. A scholarship, a job, or a personal relationship might be jeopardized by a lack of manners. The most difficult part of being a parent is that children learn from example...the ball is in your court.

Young children's manners are linked to their behavior. While preschool children might be limited to a few "rules" of etiquette, when a child is old enough to communicate, you can begin teaching simple manners. Learning to use "please" and "thank you" is a good place to start. Developing behavior that encourages good manners takes training yourself as well as your child.

Home

Even very young children should have family responsibilities. They can pick up their toys, help gather laundry, and assist with kitchen chores. Just getting cleaned and dressed in the morning is a contribution. They should be taught to respect other family members and their property.

Adult Responsibilities

Grammar and Speech

Communicate with your children using proper grammar. Your children spend five years with you before they begin their formal education, and they will mimic your speech patterns. Avoid using vulgar language, teach them the proper terms for their urinary and bowel functions, and avoid making stereotypical judgments.

Discipline

For "no" to be used effectively with small children, parents must be consistent. "No" should mean no, not maybe. Use of "the look" or "the voice" can be just as effective in discipline. My husband only had to clear his throat to make his daughters pay attention. I employed the withering look, implying "this is your last chance."

Time out is a popular form of discipline. The theory is that the child is put in a quiet corner and left to reflect on his transgressions for a certain period of time. Young children usually have no concept of time, so using a kitchen timer is helpful.

Morality

Children need to know that they are responsible for their actions. Parents must maintain values that support a moral lifestyle:

honesty, respect for everyone, and a sense of obligation to do your best. I once told my daughter that being nice to people was more important than one's physical presence in church. I was quoted some twenty years later in a graduate school paper. Sometimes children actually do listen.

Anger

When younger children have a tantrum, you can often diffuse their anger by diverting their attention. Teach them constructive ways to channel their anger by talking, drawing, or acting out their anger with puppets. It is important to control your reactions to their anger and assure them that they are loved even when you are unhappy with them.

Rewards

If you are working on a particular manner or trying to modify a behavior, a chart of your child's progress is often helpful. The child should help decide the reward. Use stickers to mark success in a particular activity. Keep your chart in a highly visible location and chart for short periods of time.

Adult Names

Children should be taught not to use an adult's first name. They should always refer to an adult as Mr., Mrs., or Ms. The use of "Sir" and "Ma'am" in response to a question is a Southern tradition. In other parts of the country it is considered a disrespectful response, and in this politically correct world, it denotes a servile meaning that is not appropriate. An adult's name (Mr. Brown) can be used in its place.

Table Manners

Children should use a napkin and dinner utensils correctly. They should not talk with food in their mouth and should ask to be excused from the dinner table following the meal. Teach them to decline food gracefully, saying, "No thank you." Toys should not be brought to the table, nor should food be played with as if it were a toy. Caps and hats are never worn at the table. (Specific dining instructions are in the adult section.)

Proper nutrition is important for children. Having a daughter who thought ketchup qualified as a vegetable, I know getting your family to eat properly is not an easy task. Teach your children which foods are nutritious and how they help bodies grow strong. Try offering an either-or option. ("Would you rather have peas or carrots?") To learn a lesson in compromise, read *Gregory the Terrible Eater* with your child.

If unacceptable behavior occurs in the home that cannot be verbally corrected, escort the child to another room and say he or she will not be allowed back at the table until the behavior is modified. This works well unless you have served some slimy green vegetable and your child does not relish the idea of returning to the table. Be sure to mention what you are having for dessert. It usually brings a child around.

When dining at a restaurant, children should not be allowed to roam the facilities or peer over the booth at the patrons behind them. If children get restless, use a small toy or book to distract them. If they start to cry, head to the restroom. When our daughters were young, we would always dine early, when the restaurants were less crowded and the service faster. While dining with our two-year-old one evening, she surprised the waiter and us by looking at her menu and declaring indignantly, "Two dollars and seventy-five cents for a hamburger?"

Resources

There are numerous books targeted for children that reinforce good manners. Among them are:

P   *The Berenstain Bears Forget Their Manners* (Berenstain)
P-2 *Modern Manners for Little Monsters* (Rogers)
P-2 *What Do You Do, Dear?* (Joslin)
P-2 *Say the Magic Word, Please* (Ross)
3-6 *Soup Should Be Seen, Not Heard* (Brainard, Behr & Behr)
4-8 *Social Smarts: Manners for Today's Kids* (James)
       Lambchop in the Land of No Manners —video

My husband and I had the good fortune to raise two loving and successful daughters. I am asked many times what we did when they were young to nurture and encourage them. My advice to parents is always the same. Take a very active interest in your children's schooling, teach them to be sensitive to the emotional needs of others, and train them to be organized. Teaching your children to be good and voracious readers is the best gift you can give them.

"Sandwich every bit of criticism between
two heavy layers of praise."

Mary Kay Ash

The Restless Years

If you happen to be in the age bracket from five to eighteen, this is the section for you. I know you are asking yourself, "What in the world does a five-year-old have in common with an eighteen-year-old?" but trust me. Etiquette is like the United States Constitution. It's a giant umbrella that covers the nation's varying citizenry. It applies equally to all.

General Manners

Please

Use this word frequently. Someone told me when I was young that "please" was a magic word. It is true. Use it frequently and you will see the magic yourself.

Interrupting

Always say "excuse me" if you interrupt someone. It should be an emergency. Otherwise, wait your turn.

Sitting and Standing

Now I have to change the way I sit? Of course you know better than to slouch in your chair, but women in social situations should sit with their knees touching and their feet flat on the floor or crossed at the ankles. I cannot tell you how many school programs I have attended where the entire audience could tell what color underwear the females sitting on stage were wearing.

Your posture is equally important. Hunched over shoulders not only look terrible, but also can permanently affect your posture. Believe me, the world admires height (think of models and athletes), so stand straight and tall.

Phone Manners

🐛 Identify yourself when making a call.

🐛 If you get a wrong number, say you are sorry and tell them the number and person you were trying to reach.

🐛 Always say "good-bye" before hanging up.

🐛 Do not yell to someone in the next room that he or she has a phone call.

🐛 Leave a clear message, including your phone number, on an answering machine.

🐛 Be sure to take complete messages, including name and phone number.

🐛 Know how to use 911.

🐛 Do not make prank calls; people have caller ID and your calls can be traced. Besides, it is very impolite.

🐛 Do not talk on the phone when you have company. Get off the phone quickly and call the person back after your company leaves.

When You Are a Guest

- Never ask for food or drinks, except water.
- Respect the rules of the home.
- Greet the parents when you arrive.
- Thank your friend's parents when you leave.
- Clean up after playing.
- If you are fed a meal, offer to help with the preparation and cleanup.
- If you are invited on a trip or for an extended stay, you may take a small hostess gift, but you *must* write a thank-you to your hostess. Thank-you notes are always addressed to the hostess (female), rather than the host (male), unless there was no hostess.

Introductions

Never, never, never use an adult's first name. All adults should be addressed as Mr., Mrs., or Ms. (pronounced miz). You may only use an adult's first name if he or she is your relative, as in Aunt Mary or Uncle Joe.

Get comfortable with introducing yourself to others.

"Hi, I'm Dani." or "Hello, my name is Susan Wright."

Order of introduction

Mention the older person first, the woman before the man, or the girl before the boy.

"Mrs. Green, I would like you to meet my brother, Scott."

"Penny, this is my best friend, Jerry."

It is really helpful to mention something about the person you are introducing.

"Coach Smith, this is my sister, Kimmy. She is entering her first marathon this week."

Now you have given Coach Smith something to talk about with your sister.

Thank You, Written and Otherwise

"Thank you." Be sure to say it often. You always like to be appreciated and so does everyone else.

You must write a thank-you note for all gifts you receive unless you are having a birthday party and open your presents in front of your guests. You still need to thank each person orally after you open a gift.

It is never wrong to write and thank someone for a gift, even if he or she saw you open it. Use clean writing paper and your best handwriting. Did you notice I did not say you could use the computer? Thank-you notes should *always* be handwritten with blue or black ink.

If you are too young to write an entire letter, draw a thank-you picture and sign your name. Grandmothers really like that kind of thing. For those of you who are over six years of age, your note should contain the following parts:

October 23, 20-- (date)

Dear Grandma, (greeting)

Your package arrived last week, but Mom made me wait until my birthday to open it. Was I surprised!

I can't believe that you were able to find a blue sweater to replace the one that I lost. I know you must have spent a lot of time trying to locate another one and I really appreciate it. Thank you for making my birthday so special. (body)

Love,   (closing)
Connie   (signature)

Thank-you notes should be more than one line. Mention the gift you received (but not the amount of money or a check) and what you plan to do with it. Thank the person. You should have three or four sentences.

Do not put smiley faces or x's and o's on your notes unless you are writing to a close friend.

Remember, if you do not write a note, how will the person who sent you a gift know you received it? Maybe they will just quit sending you gifts.

Stationery

Children

Children's stationery comes in several sizes, usually 4" x 5½" or 4" x 5" fold-over notes or 7¼" x 5¾" sheets. Thermographed, embossed, or printed stationery is fine for children, but they should not use engraved stationery. It is more appropriate to use their name rather than a monogram. *Pen Pals* and *Crayons* offer a variety of children's stationery products.

Most enclosure cards for children measure 3½" x 2" (although the correct size is 2¼" x 1⅜") and may contain their full name for a formal card, or first and last name on an informal card. Never use a title (that is, Mr., Ms., or Master) on a child's card.

Cute camp notes with postcards, sheets, and envelopes as well as stickers are available. If your children are going to camp, you might pre-address and stamp some envelopes to encourage them to write.

Avoid fill-in-the-blank thank-you notes. They are as insulting as not writing a note.

Adult

Stationery Monograms

A monogram for Mary Alice Smith may be written in one of two ways:

MAS   or   **MSA**

The correct monogram for John Robert McGuire (no space between Mc and Guire):

JRM   or   **JMR**

If the last name is two separate words, as in Alice Lynn Vander Lust then one uses four initials: **ALVL**

In the case of Ignacio Ramos De La Garza, the initials would be **IRDLG**.

Women

Women should use fold-over notes (3½" x 5") in ecru or white. They may be embossed, engraved, or thermographed with your initials or full name. They are used to reply to formal invitations (such as a wedding) or for short messages. They may also be used for thank-you notes. The front side of the note should contain your monogram (initials) or your name. Your note should begin on page three. Do not write on the back of the card.

Your name should be written: **Mary Alice Smith** (with no title).

Correspondence cards are used for thank-you notes and informal invitations or just writing a short note. They are white or ecru and measure 6¼" x 4½" and are heavier stock than fold-over notes. Your monogram or full name appears at the top (embossed, thermographed, or engraved) and the outside edge of the card may be banded in a color such as navy or dark green. You should write only on the front of the card.

Your return address should be written on the flap of the envelope (not on the front) and should just include your address, not your name.

Calling cards for a single woman should measure 2⅞" x 2". Use your full name with no title (Miss). They may be engraved or thermographed on white or ecru heavy stock. These may be used as enclosure cards for gifts (with a handwritten note on the back and signed with your casual name) or in graduation invitations.

Jennifer Lynn Harrison

Men

Men do not use fold-over notes. Correspondence cards are used for short correspondence and thank-you notes. Your name or monogram should appear at the top of the stationery.

A man's name should be written without a title.

John Smith   or   John Alan Smith

Half sheets are stationery that fold in half to fit into the envelope. They may be monogrammed or you may have your name at the top. They are used for letter writing. Blank sheets should be purchased at the same time to use as a second page. Never write on the back of this stationery. Only men may use a family crest on their stationery. The return address should be written on the envelope flap. It does not include your name.

Calling cards for men measure 3⅜" x 1½" or 3½" x 2". They may be thermographed or engraved on white or ecru card stock and should contain the full name.

Thomas Shane Ellington

At age eighteen, the title Mr. should be added. These may be used in graduation invitations and as enclosure cards for gifts. (You may write a handwritten note, signed with your casual name, on the back.)

Responding to Invitations

If the invitation says "R.S.V.P." or "please reply," it means the host wants to know in advance if you are attending. You should write or call within *two* days of receiving the invitation. They have to plan on how many guests will be there. Do not leave them guessing about how much food to prepare.

Do not discuss invitations in front of other people. No one can invite every classmate to a party. It could easily lead to hurt feelings.

If you are hosting a party, mail your invitations so that they arrive at least a week in advance of the event. You need to allow your guests enough time to reply to your invitation, as well as make any preparations to attend (buying a birthday gift or assembling the proper clothing).

Arrive at a party no later than fifteen minutes past the specified starting time, and always arrive on time if a meal is being served.

Rules, Rules, Rules

Rules and manners sometime become mixed up. If you follow the rules, you will have good manners. Here are some rules to remember.

🌑 Do not cheat.

🌑 Do not lie.

🌑 Do not swear.

Okay, I will tell this story on myself. When my children were in elementary school, I was attempting to move two science fair projects into the school before an impending rainstorm. In the process I dropped my camera. The children both insist, to this day, that I swore: something about what a beaver builds. I do not remember this at all, but it made a large impression on my children. They have not heard unmentionable language since, but they still speak in hushed tones about "the day Mother cursed."

I have a list of vulgar slang that I would like for you not to use, but I just cannot bring myself to dignify these words by putting them in print. Well, maybe just one for example: The word "butt" has crept into the vernacular, and I wish it would creep right back where it came from. The correct word is "buttock," or substitute "gluteus maximus," or "derriere," or even "rump." You certainly will sound more literate.

As rowdy as six-year-old boys can be, a group took to taunting my daughter at recess. I told her just to tell them she was "immune to their remarks." They had no idea what it meant and assumed it was something terrible. She was happy, and the harassment stopped. Intelligence rules.

Miscellaneous Items

❦ Do not chomp your gum.

❦ Do not forget to flush the toilet.

❦ Do not talk about people behind their back.

❦ Do not show off.

❦ Do not spit or pick your nose in public.

❦ Do not do something just because someone else does it.

❦ Take off your hat (yes, this means baseball caps) when you are indoors.

❦ Say "excuse me" if you burp or have gas.

So, you have read all of this and now you know not to jump on the furniture, not to take things that do not belong to you, and how to treat people respectfully...even your younger brother. You are practically perfect in every way. Now maybe you are ready to leave the house.

"Don't compromise yourself, you're all you've got."

Janis Joplin

Social Occasions

Although you may be familiar with the customs of your own family, you may be invited to participate in events with which you are unfamiliar. The more information you have beforehand, the more comfortable you will be. It is perfectly correct to ask your host or friend any questions that you may have: "What should I wear?" "What will I be expected to do?" They will be flattered that you were interested enough to inquire.

Church

Dress

If you are invited to attend a church where you are unfamiliar with the beliefs or the service, you should check with your host(ess) to determine the proper attire. Basically, women should wear skirts or dresses, and young men should wear slacks and shirts with older men wearing sport coats or suits.

Head coverings for women are not required in most Christian churches, including Roman Catholic, but are required in certain Jewish sects and in Islamic mosques. Men are required to wear a yarmulke, pronounced yáh ma ka (a small, close fitting cap), at many Jewish services, but these should be available as you enter the temple. Women attending Hindu or Islamic services should not have bare arms or skirts that do not cover their knees.

You should not wear religious symbols (i.e., crosses, etc.) when attending a religious service of another faith.

Ritual

Usually, you may sit wherever you wish. Ushers may be available to escort you to a seat. You do not take their arm, but merely follow them. The female is seated first. As others enter the pew, you should move down rather than having people step across you. If you are attending a wedding, however, you remain where you were seated. (See Weddings for more information.) Men and women are segregated at Islamic services. Women will either sit in a room to the side or at the back of the mosque, behind the men.

If you are unfamiliar with the service, you should try to follow along with the members. You may either kneel or remain seated when prayers are offered. You should always stand when the congregation does (as a gesture of respect for their religion) even if you are not participating in the ceremony. Feel free to sing or read text with the congregation if you are comfortable doing so.

Communion

Communion is basically the serving of bread and wine (or grape juice) representing the body and blood of Jesus. It may be referred to as Holy Communion, The Lord's Supper, or the Eucharist. In each church, Communion reflects the particular belief of that congregation or denomination. Catholics believe that the bread and wine becomes the actual body and blood of Christ when they are consecrated during the service. You should not participate in Communion in a Catholic church unless you are Catholic. Other religions may invite you to participate in Communion even if you are not a member.

Communion may be served at the front of the church or may be passed among the pews. You should partake in this part of the service *only* if you have been invited to do so and you wish to.

Otherwise, remain seated or pass the Communion tray without participating.

Offerings and Donation Boxes

Many churches collect an offering during the service. You do not need to give any money to this collection, but you may donate between one and five dollars. If there is no collection during the service, there will most likely be a donation box in the entry. You may make a donation there if you wish.

First Communions

In the Catholic Church, children have their first Communion when they are six or seven. Boys wear dark suits and white shirts with a tie, and girls wear white dresses and some sort of head covering. A reception or meal may follow. Guests should wear church attire and bring a gift that is religious in nature.

Confirmations

Confirmations are religious ceremonies in which children between the ages of ten and thirteen affirm their faith. The Catholic Church follows this sacrament, as well as some Protestant churches. If you are invited to a Confirmation, you are not required to give a gift, but you may take a small present that is religious in nature. If you are unfamiliar with the ceremony, just follow along the best you can and participate in the parts that are in keeping with your own religious beliefs.

Jewish Initiation

A Bar (for boys) or Bat (for girls) Mitzvah is a Jewish ceremony that usually takes place near the thirteenth birthday and involves a reading of Scriptures. At most synagogues, men are provided with a yarmulke (small cap) to wear. Women should dress modestly. Some sects require a head covering as well as the covering of arms and legs (to the knee). If the event takes place on the Sabbath (Saturday), guests should not carry anything into the ceremony, including purses. Many times a party or dinner will be held in conjunction with the event. Money ($50+) is an appropriate gift and should be sent to the home.

As with weddings, technically anyone in the congregation may attend the ceremony in the temple or synagogue. The initiation is usually followed by a small, on site reception. Any celebration beyond that is by invitation only. This may be in the form of an informal note or a formal and elaborate invitation. (See Wedding Invitations for addressing information and reply cards.)

Informal invitation:

> *Please join us Saturday, the fifteenth of November, at our daughter Elizabeth's Bat Mitzvah. It will be held at eleven o'clock at Congregation Bethel. We look forward to seeing you there.*

Formal:

> ## Mr. and Mrs. Raymond Allen Weisenfeld
> *invite you*
> *to worship with them*
> *at the Bat Mitzvah of their daughter*
>
> *Elizabeth Elaine*
>
> *Saturday, the fifteenth of November*
> *Two thousand ten*
> *at eleven o'clock*
>
> **Congregation Bethel**
> *(address if big city)*
>
> | *Reception at eight o'clock* | or | *Luncheon Reception* |
> | *Rosepoint Country Club* | | *immediately following services* |

Enclosure card:

An enclosure card may be sent with the general invitation to the ceremony for those who are invited to an additional celebration.

> *Please join us*
> *for a Dinner Dance*
> *honoring*
> *Elizabeth Elaine Weisenfeld*
> *Saturday, the fifteenth of November*
> *at eight o'clock*
> *Rosepoint Country Club*

Buddhist Initiation

A ceremony known as Jukai is performed in some Buddhist sects. There is no set age at which this takes place, but it also serves as a naming ceremony. Guests sit on cushions on the floor of the temple. It may be followed by a small reception. Alcohol is not served. No gifts are expected.

Muslim Initiation

"Taking Shahada" is witnessed by eight females or two male Muslims. It usually occurs during the teen years and may take place in a home or mosque. Guests should plan to arrive in advance of the ceremony, and they will be directed where to sit. For females, the head, arms, and the legs to below the knee should be covered. No receptions are held following the event, and no gift is expected.

Scouting

Fees for scouting include uniforms, badges, handbooks, dues, and camp expenses.

Indian Guides and Indian Princess

Indian Guides and Indian Princesses were started by Joe Friday and Harold Keltner in 1926. The program is affiliated with the YMCA. Membership is open to children in kindergarten through third grade and their fathers. Indian folklore and values are taught and there are outings and camp outs. Tribes usually consist of six to ten children and their fathers. They meet monthly. Fees range from $35, and some financial aid may be available.

Girl Scouts

Juliette Gordon Low founded the Girl Scouts in 1912. Its purpose is to meet the educational, psychological, and social needs of its members.

Daisy – kindergarten
Brownie – first through third grade
Junior – fourth through sixth grade
Cadette – seventh through ninth grade
Senior – ninth through twelfth grade

Boy Scouts

The Boy Scouts was founded in 1910 by W. D. Bryce. Its goals are to build character, develop citizenship, and stress physical fitness.

Tiger Cub – first grade
Cub Scout – ages eight through ten
Webelos Scout – fourth and fifth grade
Boy Scout – ages eleven through seventeen
Varsity Scout – ages fourteen through seventeen
Explorer – men and women eighth grade through age twenty

Camp Fire Boys and Girls

Founded in 1910 by Luther and Charlotte Gulick, Camp Fire was originally for girls, but the membership expanded to include boys in 1975. The clubs stress self-reliance and regard for the environment and provide childcare and mentoring. Programs are available from birth to age twenty-one.

Summer Camp

I was packed off to church camp in Oklahoma shortly after I moved to Texas. I rode for thirteen hours in an overcrowded Volkswagen bus, with people I did not know, only to be deposited in an unairconditioned cabin complete with scorpions. "Camp" is not a word that conjures up warm memories. I used to threaten my children with summer camp if they did not behave. Little did I know that all over Texas, excited children of all ages were eagerly hoping to attend the camp of their choice.

Applying

One does not just go to camp, one applies. Major camps in Texas require an interview and/or a recommendation. It certainly would not hurt if generations of your family attended the same camp. There are camps located throughout Texas, but the Hill Country is Mecca to Texas campers. Names like *Heart O' the Hill, Kickapoo Kamp, Longhorn, Mystic,* and *Waldemar* ring in the heads of the female population. Longhorn is the only one that also offers a camp just for boys. The camps vary in size from about one to three hundred campers per session. Some offer a short session, but most sessions last thirty days.

Expenses

A full session of summer camp hovers around the $2,500+ mark. Additional expenses include travel, insurance, fees for certain sports, clothing, and a deposit at the camp store. Some camps issue special uniforms or T-shirts to be worn during ceremonies.

Packing

There may be restrictions as to the trunk size, but all camps require that you put your name with indelible ink or iron-on name labels on each item you bring to camp. The camps do offer a laundry service. Although the list varies, the following is a general guide.

Linens

Four towels and washcloths, a pillow, two twin sheet sets and cases, two blankets or one blanket and one bedspread, two laundry bags, and two beach towels.

Clothing

Two bathing suits, water shoes and goggles, etc., bathrobe and slippers, two gowns or pajamas, ten bras, pairs of socks, and underwear, etc., two to three pairs of jeans for horseback riding, two casual dresses, ten pairs of shorts (the color may be specified), ten shirts, two pair of tennis shoes and one pair of boots for riding, rain gear, hat or cap, and a sweatshirt or light jacket.

Personal

Sunscreen, personal hygiene items, toothbrush and paste, deodorant, soap, shampoo, plastic cup, tissues, hair dryer, curling iron, and hair items.

Miscellaneous Extras

Costumes for skits, camp uniform, fan (battery or electric), flashlight, extension cord, camera and film, stationery, stamps and pens, books, and sports equipment for tennis or golf, etc.

Closing Ceremonies

The closing ceremonies for camp may last from two hours to two days, depending on the camp. Camp Longhorn's is fairly brief, and Camp Mystic's is notoriously long. Families are expected to attend.

Cotillions

Cotillions can be a variety of social gatherings, usually established for some type of dancing. There are national cotillions, such Jon D. Williams Cotillions. They travel to different cities teaching social etiquette and ballroom dancing, usually to fifth and sixth graders. There are also local groups that are formed to offer teens an opportunity to have social contact and dance instruction in a controlled environment. These cotillions are usually by invitation, but in some communities these activities are available to anyone. There is usually a fee involved.

Each cotillion has its own rules, but generally speaking they include the following:

- ❦ Be on time.
- ❦ Dress in appropriate attire. Most groups have dress codes.
- ❦ You must dance with anyone who asks you.
- ❦ If you are disruptive, you will not be allowed to attend further dances.
- ❦ You are not allowed to have dates.

Quinceañera

A quinceañera is an Hispanic religious and social celebration marking the passage of a female child to womanhood. It takes place on or near her fifteenth birthday. Her best male friend serves as her escort, and fourteen other couples, consisting of friends and relatives, compose her court and represent the past fourteen years of her life. (When the word quinceañera is capitalized, it refers to the honoree, and when the word is lowercase it refers to the celebration.)

At the reception or dance following the religious service, her flat shoes are exchanged for heels, and she dances the first dance with her father. Then her father turns her over to her escort. Friends and family provide gifts and sponsor different aspects of the reception.

Invitations

The invitation may include pictures, a list of sponsors, court members, and escort. It may also include a statement or prayer from the honoree. A separate invitation to the reception or dance may be enclosed as a "ticket" for admission.

I
Manuela Luna,
together with my parents
Tomás and Lucinda Luna,
request the honour of your presence
at a Mass of Thanksgiving
in celebration of my
Fifteenth Birthday
where I shall express my feelings before God
on becoming a young lady
Saturday, the fifteenth of July
at twelve o'clock
Mission Valdéz Catholic Church
1672 Main Street
Midland, Texas

Reception following Mass

The list of court members:

Manuela Marie Luna
Quinceañera
Escorted by Roberto Avenas

Court of Honor

(list female names)   (list male names)
Damas   *Chambelanes*

Dama de honor, or maid of honor, may be a sister or best friend. Chambelán de honor, or honor escort, is the Quinceañera's escort.

Sponsor and gift list:

Padrinos de Regalos

Bible   *Mr. and Mrs. Vincente Padilla*
Dress   *Mr. and Mrs. Arturo Villa*
Bouquet   *Mrs. Hermán García, grandmother*
Cake   *Mr. and Mrs. Herbert Hill*
Invitations *Mr. and Mrs. Alex Enríquez*
Church   *Mr. and Mrs. Fernando Hernández*

Padrinos de Baile

Mr. and Mrs. Mario Achoa
Mr. and Mrs. Roberto García
Mr. and Mrs. Ted Hurta
Mr. and Mrs. David Jalina
Mr. and Mrs. Edgar Paredes
Mrs. Emilio Rodríguez
Mr. and Mrs. Rodney Valdez

Enclosure card for dance:

Quinceañera Dance
honoring

Manuela Luna

Saturday, the fifteenth of July
Crosswinds Ballroom
1411 North Hector

8 o'clock until midnight

Please present at door   *Admit two*

If no church service is to be held, the invitation may read:

Mr. and Mrs. Tomás Elda Luna
request the pleasure of your company
at a dinner and dance
celebrating the fifteenth birthday
of their daughter

Manuela Marie

Saturday, the fifteenth of July
at eight o'clock
Crosswinds Ballroom
1411 North Hector
Midland, Texas

The invitation may be printed in English, Spanish, or bilingually. There may be an additional charge for printing in a language other than English.

The invitation may be issued by the parents, the Quinceañera, or jointly.

Addressing Invitations

Invitations should have an inner and outer envelope. They should be addressed in the same manner wedding invitations are addressed, using no abbreviations except Mr. and Mrs. and Sr. and Sra. (See Wedding Invitations for complete instructions.)

Responsibilities of the Court

- You will need to learn any presentation dances and attend all rehearsals.
- You will need to pay for your clothes and shoes.
- There may be some form of religious preparation as well as a church rehearsal.
- You need to buy a gift for the Quinceañera.

Sponsors

The head of the family asks friends and relatives to be sponsors. They are usually expected to donate $50-$100 in goods or cash to pay for some aspect of the celebration. They may offer to pay more or may bear the total cost for the cake or some other item. The main donors may also be asked to take part in the church procession. If you ask people to help with your daughter's quinceañera, you are obligated to return the favor when their daughter has her quinceañera. If finances are a problem, offer your time to help cook, decorate, or make the capias (favors).

The Church Service

A quinceañera is not a sacrament in the Catholic Church, but a declaration of faith. Still, there are certain religious requirements that must be fulfilled before the ceremony. The service is usually held on the same day as the party and may or may not include a mass. Check with the priest to see if he will agree to say a mass. Also, inquire if the church will print a program and if there are any fees involved. Be sure to schedule a rehearsal time.

The court may be required to attend religious classes or attend a retreat.

Some Protestant churches have created their own quinceañera services.

The Ceremony

The ceremony will vary with the church, but there are usually Bible readings, hymns, a processional and recessional. Members of the court should arrive at the church an hour before the ceremony to dress and have pictures taken. Traditionally, Catholics place a bouquet of roses at the altar of the Virgin Mary.

The Theme

Usually a theme is selected along with a color. This can be an elaborate theme that is carried out through the presentation and dancing or just indicated by the decorations. The color of one's birthstone is often selected as the theme color.

Dress

The dress should be something appropriate for church. (No cleavage or bare backs and the arms should be covered.) The dresses are usually white or pastel with gloves and headpieces of flowers or pearls completing the ensemble. Flats may be worn during the church service, and the Quinceañera may change into heels as part of the ceremony. Female members of the court wear matching dresses, and the male members normally wear tuxedos.

Capias and Doll

A replica doll of the Quinceañera in her dress is often displayed at the dance. The doll is covered in ribbon favors called capias. The favors have the Quinceañera's name and date of her party. They are passed out to everyone who attends the dance. Additional favors pertaining to the theme of the quinceañera may also be placed on the tables.

Dinner

The order of events is usually the dinner (if you choose to have one), the presentation, and the dance. The Quinceañera sits in the center of the head table, with her mother on her right and her father on her left. Other family members may be seated there also.

A brindis, or toast, is offered to the Quinceañera. She, in turn, thanks her family and friends. (See Toasting.) The birthday cake is traditionally a yellow cake with a fruit filling.

Grand March

La Marcha, or grand march, is a procession of the family, court, and patrons that takes place before the presentation. It is followed by the presentation of the Quinceañera, any choreographed dances, and finally, the waltz with her father and a bow to the guests.

Gifts

This is a birthday celebration. Gifts or cash in envelopes should be taken to the dance and placed on the appropriate table. Presents are not opened at the party but usually on the following day.

Legal Implications

If you are planning to serve alcohol, you are legally responsible if someone leaves the party and is involved in an accident. Since you will be entertaining a large number of minors, this is especially important. You may ask your insurance agent about purchasing a policy to cover you for the event. Also, be sure to provide rides for those who have had too much to drink.

Musicians, Rentals, Video, and Photography

(See Weddings.)

Thank-You Notes

Thank-you scrolls tied with ribbons may be given to each guest.
The following is an example.

> *Your presence at my*
> *fifteenth birthday*
> *meant so much to me.*
>
> *Thank you for sharing*
> *this special memory.*
>
> *Fondly,*
>
> *Yolanda*

Patrons should receive handwritten thank-you notes and all
gifts should be acknowledged with a handwritten thank-you.
Never mention the amount of a check or cash gift. Thank-you
notes should be written with blue or black ink on white or ecru
fold-over notes. Write only on the third page of these notes. Your
return address, but not your name, should be written on the back
flap of the envelope.

> *June 20, 20–*
>
> *Dear Aunt Helene,*
>
> *I was so excited when I opened your*
> *gift. Your generous check will be*
> *used to buy a printer for my computer.*
>
> *Now I will be able to print out all my*
> *homework at home.*
>
> *Thank you for attending my celebration*
> *and remembering me in such a special way.*
>
> *Sincerely,*

Men, are you feeling left out? Some areas have initiated
Beau parties... the male counterpart of a Quinceañera.

Dating

The exact age at which you are allowed to begin dating is determined by your parents. If you are at an age where you wish to do things socially and your parents are against a date, as such, you should consider getting a group of your friends together to attend a movie or other activity. It will give your parents a chance to see that you can interact with the opposite sex in a responsible way, and it will take a lot of pressure off of you. Plan these activities well in advance so no one feels as if he or she was included as a last resort.

Except for Sadie Hawkins or Turn About dances, most of the dating in high school is initiated by the male. I am approaching the topic from that point of view.

Asking Someone Out

Ask your date a week in advance, unless it is a spur of the moment activity. If it is a formal event, you should invite someone three to four weeks ahead of time.

Be sure to specify the type of dress: casual, church clothes, or formal.

Give all the pertinent information, such as time and place, if you are planning to double date, and who will be transporting you.

Refusing

If you do not wish to go out with a particular person, you may decline by saying, "Thank you for asking me, but I already have plans." Remember, if you turn down one date, you should not accept another date (later) for the same evening. If you already have plans but *want* to go out with this person, give them some clues. "I would love to go, but I have to attend my aunt's wedding Friday night. I've really been dying to see that movie...."

The Date

🌱 Be on time.

🌱 Greet the parents and tell them what your plans are for the evening and when you will be home. If there is a curfew conflict, settle it before you leave the house.

🌱 Go around to her side and open the car door for your date. Be sure to open it when you get where you are going, too.

🌱 Offer your hand to help her get out of the car. She may be a star athlete, but getting out of an automobile in a tight fitting formal is no easy feat.

🌱 Do not drink if you are driving. Do not let others drink in your car because you (as the driver) will be legally responsible if the police stop you.

🌱 Introduce your date to your friends.

🌱 Plan your finances ahead of time. Make a rough estimate of what the evening will cost and be sure to carry some additional money for a cushion. Do not forget you need to leave a tip at the restaurant, and you could have to pay to park at some places or tip the valet parking service. Coat check will eat up another dollar and on it goes. Planning ahead will keep you from being caught short. If you are double dating, check with the other guy to make sure he has thought his finances through, also.

Probably the most embarrassing date I ever had was when I was taken out to dinner at a very nice restaurant and my date paid for the dinner with a sack of coins that his mother had won playing cards. As to my choice of dates, all I can say in my defense is that I was only sixteen and he owned the best-looking convertible....

🌱 Take your date home at the specified time. Do not be late. *Always* phone if there is a problem.

❦ Be sure to escort your date to the door, and do not leave until she is safely inside. If you want to kiss your date goodnight, read the suggestions in the kissing section.

If You Are the Date

❦ Be sure you understand the attire required.

❦ Settle curfews and plans with your parents ahead of time.

❦ Be ready on time.

❦ Give your date enough time to come around and open your car door. You can sit there and wait if he does not do it, or you can get out by yourself.

❦ Always carry some form of identification.

❦ Take money for a pay phone. Call your parents if your date is drinking or making you uncomfortable or threatening your safety. Do not worry about what your parents will think. They will be happy that you had the good sense to call them.

❦ Pay attention to your date. Do not flirt with other guys.

❦ Thank your date when he takes you home.

❦ Be home on time. Call if there is a problem.

Kissing

There probably is not anyone who does not remember his/her first kiss. According to Dr. Joyce Brothers, women kiss about eighty different men before they are married. So sooner or later you will come up against the good, the bad, and the ugly of kissing. Here are a few guidelines to help you.

❦ Kissing in public, other than a brief greeting, is yucky. No one is interested in your love life, so keep it out of the mall.

❦ If you want to kiss someone, be sure to approach in a nonthreatening way. If you slowly lower your face to hers and she pulls away, that's your clue to *stop*. Remember the first grader who was expelled from school for planting an unwanted kiss on a classmate. Never try to force an unwanted kiss on anyone.

❦ Close your eyes, close your mouth, and break off the kiss before you need oxygen.

❦ Keep your hands off any part of the body that is normally covered by a bathing suit. If you are uncomfortable about where your partner's hands are, then move them.

❦ Do not glob on the lipstick. It makes a mess.

❦ Shave. Beard stubble hurts.

❦ Do not kiss and tell. No one wants his/her kisses discussed Monday at lunch.

❦ Do not ever kiss to make someone else jealous or to mislead someone.

Remember:

> "Lots of things have been started by kisses,
> especially young things!"

Anonymous

Flowers

Mums

As long as there are football homecomings in Texas, there will be mums. You know, those huge white flowers with all the ribbons and stuff hanging off them. On a recent trip to the "mum store" I counted no less than 75 objects from which to choose. I saw a young man pick up his order, totaling $125. He was thrilled with all the attached paraphernalia and was confident that his steady girlfriend would just love it. I wondered where he was going to get the money to pay for dinner and the football game.

I could have saved him about $95 if he had just asked me. Before tossing away your life savings, it might be a good idea to inquire just what type of mum your date might like. Both my daughters had a particular aversion to a mum laden with anything more than ribbons. The weight of a "monster mum" can pull your clothes out of alignment as well as tear a hole in your clothing. A cowbell tied to the end of a streamer cut a large gash in my daughter's leg. She still bears the scar. This advice goes for the female as well. A lot of guys do not want to be walking around wearing a decorated garter on their arm.

Corsages

Corsages are usually presented at formal or semiformal occasions. White is always a safe color if you do not know what your date will be wearing. Carnations, gardenias, or sweetheart roses are nice. Be sure to order your corsage several weeks in advance, and plan to pick it up around midday on the day of the event. Then if there is any mix-up on your order, you have time to correct the mistake. Storing corsages in the refrigerator will keep them fresh. Wrist corsages seem to be favored by young women. They do not become smashed when you are dancing, and you do not have to deal with pinning them on.

Boutonnieres

Boutonnieres are usually single flowers, like a carnation or rose bud, that men wear on the left lapel of their tuxedo. Check to see if your date is wearing a colored cummerbund or bow tie and coordinate the colors. As with corsages, white is always a safe color.

Senior Year

Your last year of high school can be very busy. By the time you are a senior, you probably have lots of commitments and too little time. It is important that you are extra careful about keeping track of your social obligations. Mark your calendar and answer party invitations promptly. Also include testing dates for the SAT, ACT, achievement tests, interviews, and college visitations.

Getting Recommendations for College

Most colleges and universities require that you send recommendations along with your college application. These should be from people that you have worked for or that you have had as teachers. Depending on the competitiveness of the college, your recommendations can go a long way in selling you to the entrance committee.

If you are seeking an athletic scholarship, of course ask your coach to write a recommendation. Otherwise, select those people who know you best and will express their thoughts cohesively. Make recommendation requests early. Just remember, everyone in your graduating class is looking for three or more recommendations for a job or college. The earlier you ask, the less likely your teacher will have to rush through it.

When a teacher agrees to write a recommendation, submit a list including your academic activities, civic work, and athletic involvement. Include music and art related work and any awards you have won, including scholarships. It should also contain your class rank and grade point average. Many times recommendations must be sent directly to the college. Ask her/him to keep a copy of the recommendation in case you wish to apply somewhere else, or it becomes lost in transit. In some cases you will not be privy to the information sent.

Supply your teacher with a pre-addressed envelope, stamped with the proper postage, and a return receipt form with your address. (This costs extra, but it is well worth it.) Your teacher will turn in the letter and the form at the post office and will notify you when the college has signed for your recommendation. Think of the thousands of recommendations flying in to each college and university. Wouldn't you like to be able to say that Jane Collins had signed for your recommendation on December 15 and would they please look again?

You are not finished quite yet. Write all your recommenders a handwritten thank-you note. Their time is valuable, and you need to let them know how much you appreciate their help. (See Stationery.)

Senior Parties

Many times a party or parties will be held in honor of a graduating senior. If a luncheon or party is being held in your honor, be sure to check with your hostess as to the number of guests you should invite. Provide their names and addresses as quickly as possible. You may want to give a small gift to your hostess and be sure to write a thank-you note. If there are multiple hostesses, you need to send them each a note.

Hosting a senior party

If you wish to host a party for a graduating senior, call the parents and specify the type of party you wish to give, the number of people you can accommodate, and a date or dates from which to choose. Occasionally, there may be a group of hostesses for an event. Do not offer to act as one of the hostesses unless you plan to attend the party. If you cannot participate, you *may not* be a hostess. You may always send a gift to the graduate in lieu of hosting a party.

The names of hostesses should be listed alphabetically. Use first and last names only, no titles. For example, Mary Smith (not Mrs. John Smith). The listing of hostesses may be horizontal or vertical. An asterisk may be placed after the name of the person who is handling the replies. If the party is being held at someone's home, her name is listed first. (See Civic and Charity Events for listing of multiple hostesses.)

Jane Doe, Kathy Dumbe, and Elaine Fox

or

Susan Arthur
Jane Crixell
Amy Goff

Sample senior party invitations:

Please come to a Picnic
honoring
Sara Brown

Saturday, March 15th
twelve o'clock

Community Park

Reply
Beth Mitchell   *Rain date*
602-0301   *3/22/--*

Barbecue Dinner and Western Dance

honoring

Debbie Clyde

VFW Hall
Saturday, May thirteenth
seven o'clock

Amy and Steve Brown*   Ellen and Al Corby
Sue and Mike Goss
Betty and Chris Pine   Regina Steel

reply*
606-1122   Western dress

Graduation

High school graduation is an exciting time. It signifies a passage in life...on to college or a job. Many graduations have limited seating, and one may not attend without an invitation. Others are held in large auditoriums and are open to the public.

If you receive an invitation to a graduation, you may send a card or gift to the participant, depending on how close you are to that person. Money is always appreciated by graduates. Other suggestions are things that they might need for a new dorm or apartment. If you are unsure, you can always call the graduate's parent for suggestions. If you receive a graduation *announcement*, no response or gift is necessary.

Graduation Invitations

Mail your invitations one month prior to graduation. Send them to close friends and grandparents, only. This is not the time for a large mail-out.

Most graduation invitations are generic in nature and require that you personalize it by inserting your calling card into the invitation. Calling cards may be ordered when you order your invitations. They are printed with your full name.

Mary Alice Hernandez

Addressing Invitations

Graduation invitations have two envelopes. The larger, gummed envelope should be addressed in blue or black ink, using full names: Mr. and Mrs. William Fields. You must write out the word "and."

On the inner envelope, write the names of the recipients: Aunt Sue and Uncle Ted. Put the folded edge of the invitation into the inner envelope, with the writing on the announcement facing the back of the envelope.

Place the inside envelope into the large outside envelope with the *front* of the inner envelope facing the *back* of the outside envelope. Your return address (no name) should be written on the back flap of the outer envelope.

(See Wedding Invitations for more complete instructions on addressing formal invitations. It includes the proper forms of address for judges, politicians, doctors, and religious leaders.)

Cap and Gown

The cap should be worn so that the top (mortarboard) is level on your head and the crown is about an inch above your eyebrows. The front or back of the cap should be marked inside. Having dealt with several "hat" traumas on graduation days, I suggest that you practice with the cap and make sure it fits and that it can be anchored to the head if necessary.

Traditionally, men remove their caps during the National Anthem and their school song, but check with your school to see what their procedure is. The tassel may be worn on either side and is often moved from one side to the other as part of the graduation ceremony.

Gifts and Thank-You Notes

What fun it is to receive graduation presents! Unfortunately, now you have to write all the thank-you notes. If you are lucky, one of your gifts was some nice, plain, nonfolding stationery called correspondence cards (for men and women), which are usually white or ecru. They can be engraved, embossed, or thermographed with your initials or name. Women may also use fold-over notes. Write your note on page three of these notes, and never write on the back of the note. (See Stationery.)

Of course, thank-you notes must be handwritten in blue or black ink. Like all letters, notes contain four main parts:

(1) the greeting or salutation, beginning with "Dear_____,
(2) the main body of the note, where you mention the gift and what you are going to do with it
(3) the closing, Love, Sincerely, etc.
(4) the signature that can include only a first name if the recipient is a close friend

The date should be included in the upper right-hand corner. Your return address goes on the back flap of the envelope, but never include your name.

Sample graduation gift thank-you:

June 1, 20–

Dear Mrs. Smith,

Thank you for the gift certificate from Dillards. I am looking forward to shopping for things for my dorm room.

It certainly has been an exciting time for me. I will come by to see you before I leave for college and show you what I selected.

Sincerely,

Jane

53

"All our lives we are preparing to be something or somebody, even if we don't know it."

Kathryn Anne Porter

Out of the Nest

Deciding where you want to go to college and getting admitted is just the beginning of the Texas college experience. Sororities and fraternities are a big part of campus life. Rush is very competitive and can even be brutal. Horror stories about rush abound.

After offering to write a recommendation for the daughter of an acquaintance, the girl's mother informed me that her daughter had met some nice girls at camp and planned to be in their sorority. I tried to explain how difficult it was to pledge at the major universities, but the mother was undaunted. The daughter was ultimately cut from that particular sorority and not having any other recommendations, failed to pledge.

College Visitations

Many colleges and universities have special visitation weekends for prospective students. You may stay as the guest of a student in one of the dorms. Be sure to write a thank-you note to your host. A small basket of candy or home baked goodies would be a nice thing to take to a woman. Men seem to be much more casual about this, and you would not need to do anything but write a thank-you note. If you have an interview with a professor or administrator, be sure to write and thank him or her.

November 15, 20–

Dear Carol,

Thank you for serving as my official hostess for "Meet Us Monday." I had a wonderful tour of the campus. You introduced me to so many kind and helpful people. It really convinced me that August University is the place I'd like to spend the next four years.

I look forward to seeing you next fall.

Sincerely,

November 15, 20–

Dear Professor Hadley,

I enjoyed meeting you and discussing the requirements and internship opportunities for geology students at August University. I have shared the prospectus you gave me with my parents. We are all enthusiastic about the possibilities.

Thank you for your time and the tour of the science facilities.

Sincerely,

Sorority and Fraternity Rush

Rush is the process by which male and female students select, and are selected, to be members of various Greek organizations. Each school has its own rules concerning the time and length of rush. For more information, contact the student life office or Greek coordinator at your college.

Females

Acquaintances who are alumnae of a Greek organization may write *recommendations* (*recs*) for you for that particular group. Having a rec for each of the Greek organizations (*sororities*) on campus is a good way for them to get to know you before you start formal rush.

When someone writes a rec for you, he or she will request photos and other information. It is a good idea to type up an information sheet including your grade point average, class rank, SAT or ACT score, honors, elected offices, sports, extracurricular activities, and community service. Photos should not include any other people or animals. Be sure to write and thank anyone who wrote a rec for you.

If you are a female and wish to participate in collegiate rush, you should register with your local *Panhellenic Council*. Panhellenic provides local alumnae with your name and the college you are planning to attend. They will try to obtain recommendations for those students with a balance of good grades, extra-curricular activities, and appropriate SAT or ACT scores. There are minimum score levels set by each Greek organization.

Males

If you are a male, rush will be much simpler. Male alumni may write recommendations for you, but rush for men is less complicated. You are invited to parties at the *fraternity* (male equivalent of sorority) houses, and if you are mutually amused with each other, you will be asked to join.

The Process

Be sure *not* to discuss your preferences before rush starts: Your ideas may change when you get a good look at each organization. Keep an open mind and meet as many people as you can during rush. For women, during the first round of rush (usually two days), you are invited, at designated times, to attend a function at each of the sororities on campus.

After the first round, you will only go back to those sorority houses that send you an invitation. If you do not receive an invitation, then you have been *cut* from that sorority's list of potential new members. Once you have been cut, you will not be invited back to that house for any other parties during that rush period.

The final round is called *pref night*. After the parties that night, you will make a selection of your first choice, or first and second choice, from your final parties. The next day you will be notified if you have received a *bid* (offer to join) from the sorority you have selected. If you wish to *pledge*, accept the bid. If you do not wish to be a member, you may decline the bid. Anytime during the rush period, you may withdraw from rush.

Many campuses have "*open rush*" in which they are constantly considering candidates for their fraternity or sorority. Others hold a spring rush as well as a fall rush. Your college or university will be able to provide you with the dates of rush and a list of rules. Some colleges and universities have deferred rush, that is, they have rush the second semester or even the second year of college. Most schools hold their rush before the start of the freshman fall semester.

Some campuses have local, rather than national, fraternities or clubs.

Legacy

A legacy is the child, grandchild, or sibling of an initiated member of a fraternity or sorority.

Hazing

Hazing or any form of harassment of pledges has been outlawed by all Greek organizations and college and universities.

The Greek Alphabet

Most organizations are designated by Greek letters. The Greek alphabet is shown below.

alpha	nu
beta	xi
gamma	omicron
delta	pi
epsilon	rho
zeta	sigma
eta	tau
theta	upsilon
iota	phi
kappa	chi
lambda	psi
mu	omega

Parents and Rush

Your student will have enough adjustments to make being away from home, attending a new school, and social pressures. Do not add to her burden by inflicting your Greek preferences on your child.

First of all, things could have changed dramatically since you were a Mu Epsilon at dear old State University. Chapter personalities change with the students, and the popularity of organizations ebb and flow. Let your child make the decision if she wants to pledge and where she wants to pledge.

Before an alumnae organization or an individual sends anything to a sorority house during rush, check with your local sorority's rush chairperson. Rules and requests change frequently and vary from school to school.

If your child is a legacy and pledges your sorority, it is proper to request to participate in the initiation ceremony. Contact your child's sorority for information.

In addition to the following list, there is also a traditionally African-American Sorority and Fraternity *Pan Hellenic.*

National Panhellenic Sororities	*National Panhellenic Fraternities*
Alpha Chi Omega	Lambda Chi Alpha
Alpha Delta Pi	Lambda Theta Phi
Alpha Epsilon Phi	Lambda Phi Epsilon
Alpha Gamma Delta	Pi Kappa Alpha
Alpha Omicron Pi	Pi Kappa Phi
Alpha Phi	Pi Lambda Phi
Alpha Sigma Alpha	Sigma Alpha Epsilon
Alpha Sigma Tau	Sigma Alpha Mu
Alpha Xi Delta	Sigma Lambda Beta
Gamma Phi Beta	Sigma Nu
Delta Gamma	Sigma Pi
Delta Delta Delta	Sigma Tau Gamma
Delta Zeta	Sigma Phi Society
Delta Phi Epsilon	Sigma Phi Epsilon
Theta Phi Alpha	Sigma Chi
Kappa Alpha Theta	Tau Delta Phi
Kappa Delta	Tau Epsilon Phi
Kappa Kappa Gamma	Tau Kappa Epsilon
Pi Beta Phi	Phi Gamma Delta
Sigma Delta Tau	Phi Delta Theta
Sigma Kappa	Phi Kappa Psi
Sigma Sigma Sigma	Phi Kappa Sigma
Phi Mu	Phi Kappa Theta

National Panhellenic Sororities
  Phi Sigma Sigma
  Chi Omega

National Panhellenic Fraternities
  Phi Kappa Tau
  Phi Lambda Chi
  Phi Mu Delta
  Phi Sigma Kappa
  Chi Phi
  Chi Psi
  Psi Upsilon
  Acacia
  Farmhouse
  Triangle

"No matter how far we may wander, Texas lingers
with us, coloring our perceptions of the world."

Elmer Kelton

Debutantes and Escorts

Sometime between her sophomore and senior year in college, a woman may be presented to society in a formal ceremony. Making her "debut" was the traditional way for a young woman to find a husband. Today, it is merely an occasion that marks a woman's entrance into adult society. Debutantes (debs) are sponsored by their parents or grandparents and are presented under the auspices of the organization that holds the presentation. Each organization has its own rules and regulations pertaining to debutantes. Debs are usually required to wear white formal gowns and long kid gloves at their presentation.

Responsibilities

Your Responsibilities as a Debutante

- Follow all rules and regulations of the sponsoring organization.
- Attend all debutante parties and functions.
- Accept and regret to invitations promptly.
- Keep a list of gifts received and send thank-you notes on your correspondence cards or informals. (See Stationery.)

🐞 If someone hosts a party in your honor, a hostess gift is appropriate along with a thank-you note.

🐞 If a large group hosts a party, hostess/host gifts are not necessary, but a thank-you note should be sent to each host/hostess.

🐞 Submit your guest lists on time and make sure to have *full names* and addresses with ZIP codes.

🐞 You may need to register your dress when you make your selection to avoid duplications.

🐞 Select an escort. Some organizations require multiple escorts.

🐞 Learn the bow to be used at the presentation.

🐞 Do not drink when you are the recipient of a toast.

🐞 Prepare the appropriate toasts. (See Toasts.)

Optional:

🐞 Purchase a deb picture for the escort(s).

🐞 Escorts may be given a small gift.

Your Responsibilities as an Escort

🐞 Attend all debutante activities to which you are invited.

🐞 Accept and regret invitations promptly.

🐞 Provide names and addresses of siblings (in the college age group) and parents for invitation lists.

🐞 Check on the dress (tuxedo) requirements.

🐞 Attend the debutante presentation practice.

🐞 Prepare a short toast in honor of the debutante. (See Toasts.)

🐞 Buy a small gift for the debutante.

Your Responsibilities as a Debutante Parent

❦ Attend all planning meetings.

❦ Make sure all your invitation lists are turned in on time and in the correct form. Include full names, no abbreviations, and be sure to include ZIP codes. (See Addressing Wedding Invitations for the proper forms of address.)

❦ Pay all fees on time.

❦ Reply and regret promptly to invitations.

Fathers may be part of presentation:

❦ They need to attend all practices.

❦ They should wear the appropriate attire for the presentation.

❦ They need to prepare a toast for their daughter. (See Toasts.)

The parents may wish to give debutante a gift to mark the occasion.

Hosting a Debutante Party

Parties may be given in honor of one or more debutantes. You should check with the debutante and clear the party with her. Then call the organization that is sponsoring the deb and request a date for your party. Parties are registered to avoid duplications. Also, some organizations limit the number of parties allowed per deb. When your party has been approved, call the debutante and give her a total number of guests and a deadline for turning in her guest list. If a group is hosting a party, remember, you cannot serve as a hostess for an event unless you will be in attendance.

Legal Implications

Many of the guests and siblings attending debutante functions may be under the legal drinking age. If you serve as a host or hostess at a party, you are legally responsible if someone leaves the event intoxicated and is involved in an accident. Insurance is available to cover the hosts at such events, and although it is expensive, it is well worth it. Check your homeowner's policy to see what coverage you may already have.

Invitations

Refer to the wedding invitation chapter for correct addressing for formal invitations as well as samples of reply cards.

Mr. and Mrs. Keith Edward Smith
request the pleasure of your company
at a dance honoring their granddaughter

(Miss) Jennifer Lynn Charlesworth

Saturday, the second of December
at seven o'clock
The Briar Club
(you may list the address)

R.s.v.p.
1602 Morgan Avenue
Houston, Texas 77084

If an organization is hosting the presentation, the invitation might resemble the following.

> *The Board of Directors*
> *of the Freemont Club*
> *requests the honor of the presence of*
>
> _____ (fill in the name)
>
> *at the Debutante Presentation*
>
> *on Saturday, the twenty-seventh of December*
> *at eight o'clock*
> *Metropolitan Club*
>
> *R.S.V.P.*   *Black tie*
> *42 Ashton Lane*
> *Waco, Texas 77934*

If a group of debutante parents are issuing an invitation, the names of the debutantes could be listed on the front of the invitation and the party information listed on the third page of a folding invitation. The "Miss" may be omitted, but do not use Ms.

The parents of

(Miss) Edith May Allen
(Miss) Margaret Ethel Bowen
(Miss) Cassandra Elaine Fowler
(Miss) Jennifer Lynn Horn
(Miss) Kathleen Ray Miller
(Miss) Amanda Taylor Swift
(Miss) Ann Marie Wallace

Gifts

Only very close friends should give a debutante gift.

Lois Smitherman, Mardi Gras and debutante consultant, has generously provided the following instructions for debutante presentations.

Debutant Instructions

Flowers

Debutantes usually use a round nosegay, a cascade of flowers, or an arm spray. Your bouquet should always be presented facing the audience. Never hold your bouquet at your waist. It should be held at hip level, which lends a more relaxed look to your appearance. It also ensures that you do not block the view of the bodice of your dress, which usually is the most ornate part of your gown.

Posture

Debutantes should stand with a straight back, relaxed shoulders, and chin up. When not in motion, standing in the fourth ballet position provides a comfortable stance that allows a slight shift in weight to maintain circulation in your legs. Never lock your knees. It will restrict your movement, and you could easily faint under the heat of stage lights.

As a debutante promenades around the ballroom or stage, she should move slowly and gracefully. Lead with the ball of your foot, giving the appearance that you are gliding across the floor. Keep the movement of the hem of your gown to a minimum. Never walk in time to the music or faster than your escort. If you find yourself moving too rapidly, shorten the length of your stride. Be sure to make eye contact with your audience.

The Curtsy

Your speed on the descent and ascent, paired with your posture, will make or break your performance. The key to a successful performance is practice.

- Come to a complete stop before the bow begins. Never "walk" in or out of your bow because the risk of losing your balance is great.

- If you have an escort, leave your right hand on your escort's arm or hand and take a small step to your left, away from your escort.

- Move the right foot (closest to escort) past your left leg and just behind it. Balance your weight between the front and back legs.

- With a straight back and chin held high, begin to bend the left leg. You may go as low as sitting on your right (back) foot, but reach at least a ninety-degree angle and hold for the count of three.

- Using your thigh muscles, slowly reverse your descent. Keep your chin up and your back straight. Do not give the appearance of heaving yourself off the floor.

- Your escort will help you maintain your balance on the descent and ascent. Keep your flowers at the hip level or slightly to the side, but never extend the bouquet out to the side in a dramatic fashion.

- Once back in a standing position, pause to regain your balance, then proceed.

The "Texas Bow"

Debutantes in Tyler, Texas, are known for their French full court bow. The bow requires good knees and lots of practice. Basically, one leg is wrapped around the other, while kneeling. Then the deb lowers herself all the way to the floor. While sucking in her lips, to keep the lipstick from staining her dress, her head is lowered to the floor.

"No experience is a bad experience unless
you gain nothing from it."

Lyndon Johnson

Getting a Job

So you have graduated from high school, college, or technical school and you need to find a job and support yourself. No fair moving home. We have already converted your bedroom to a sewing room.

The Resume

In order to get a job, you need a resume. A resume is a list of your personal information, as well as your educational history and job experience. There are many books and computer programs that can help you develop a good resume. *Never* exaggerate your work or educational experience. Companies will call your former employers and check your references. The fastest way to lose a job is to be caught in a lie. (See the sample cover letter and resume.)

The Interview

Have a friend ask you practice questions before the interview. Be on time. Take samples of your work, if applicable. Be familiar with the business so you can discuss it intelligently with the interviewer. Be confident in your abilities. Stress your strong points, but do not be boastful. Look at the interviewer when speaking.

Thank the interviewer for his or her time, and follow up with a written thank-you. You should write and mail your thank-you note the day of your interview.

Dress Appropriately

Dress according to the type of job for which you are interviewing. Do a little scouting to see what the other people in the workplace are wearing or ask the person who sets up the interview what would be appropriate to wear. No matter what, be clean and neat, and iron your clothes. (I am sure someone has an iron you could borrow.)

What if They Take Me to Lunch?

Horrors! Now don't you wish you had paid attention when your mother told you which fork to use? This would be a good time to read the chapter on dining etiquette. Many job opportunities are lost due to the applicant's bad table manners. Here are some extra tips for you when you are dining with your prospective boss.

You will usually have to order first, being the guest. Select something in the mid-price range from the menu.

Consider how difficult (messy) it is to eat...ribs, etc. Do not order an appetizer unless your host suggests it. Then order salad or soup and a main dish. If you have not read the chapter on table manners, work from the outside in on your silverware and use the glasses on your right. *Drink right, eat left.* Do not smoke or order drinks. When you are finished eating, place your knife and fork across your plate on a diagonal and set your napkin on the table to your left. (See Dining.)

If they invite you to lunch, they pay. I hope you are able to relax enough to enjoy the free meal.

Business Cards

🍒 Business cards are imprinted on white or ecru heavy stock paper (3½" x 2") with black or gray ink.

🍒 Your business cards should include your name, title, and the name of the company as well as your address, phone, fax, and e-mail address. Keep them in a cardholder so that they remain neat and clean.

🍒 The style of your card should be in keeping with your type of business.

🍒 More creative and less formal cards are appropriate for nonprofessional businesses.

🍒 Offer your card before a meeting starts. If you are mailing pamphlets or brochures, you may attach your business card. They may also be enclosed with business gifts.

🍒 Do not pass out your cards during a meal. If you must give out your card at a social function, do so discreetly.

Sample business card:

Michael William Thomas
Chief Financial Officer

Maybridge Technology

211 Hunter Avenue   (915) 681-0001
Midland, Texas 79701   mas@mtech.com

Office Etiquette

Shaking Hands

Sounds simple enough...just put out your right hand and shake. Use a firm but not crushing grip, using the full hand. You may offer your hand to anyone to whom you have been newly introduced (man or woman). A handshake may also be used as a greeting or good-bye to friends.

If someone has a disability, it is acceptable to offer the left hand for a handshake.

Returning Phone Calls

Telephone calls, e-mail, and faxes should all be acknowledged on the day they are sent.

Pagers and Cell Phones

Pagers and cell phones are helpful in business, but shut them off during meetings and social engagements.

Opening Office Doors

I bet you are thinking career opportunity here, but what I am talking about is opening and holding doors for others. Office doors are nonsexual. They should be opened and held for anyone with an armful of files, etc. It is a good idea not to slam the door in your boss' face, either. Holding the door for someone is the polite thing to do. Outside the office, it's ladies first, but at work all men and women are created equal.

Titles for Women in Business

The title Ms. is appropriate for all women in business. If you prefer to use Mrs., you should use your first name rather than your husband's: Mrs. Mary Brown. This is *only* appropriate in a business situation and never used socially, as that indicates the woman is divorced.

Tipping

Business means dining out, entertaining clients, and traveling. Here are some suggested guidelines for tipping.

These people get fifteen percent or more: (Texas sales tax can usually be doubled to get a ballpark figure.)

Waiter or waitress, wine steward, room service, bartender, taxi driver, barber, or beauty shop stylist. It is proper to tip the owner of a hair salon.

These people get a dollar:

Coat check, bellhop (per bag), skycap (per 2 bags), chambermaid (per night), manicurist (for simple manicure, more for acrylics or tips), and valet.

Of course, this is predicated on the fact that you are happy with the service they provided. Sometimes a service charge is already added to your bill, such as room service. You do not need to add an additional tip. If you have outstanding service, you can always increase the size of the tip.

Sample cover letter:

1307 Rocky Lane
Eden, Texas 78706
February 23, 20–

Mr. Joseph Hammond
Personnel Director
Worldwide Accounting
3204 Memory Lane
Dallas, Texas 78796

Dear Mr. Hammond,

The focus of my studies at Blank University has been accounting and the related fields of economics and finance. I have worked in payroll and bookkeeping as well as preparing financial statements for Blank University. Having lived abroad as a young child, I am fluent in both Spanish and French and have tutored these languages at the college level. I have also taught computer literacy courses for the past five years. Working with students, I have developed strong interpersonal and organizational skills.

My career objectives coincide with the recent merger and expansion of your company into foreign markets. I would be interested in a position in one of your overseas offices. Please contact me at (409) 777-0203.

Sincerely,

Cheryl Lyle

enc. resume

Sample resume:

Cheryl Ann Lyle
1307 Rocky Lane
Eden, Texas 78706
(409) 777-0203

Career Objective
    To secure an entry-level position in a global accounting firm.

Summary of Qualifications
    Course work in accounting and related fields of economics and
        finance
    Multilingual: French, Spanish and English
    Excellent computer skills, knowledge of current accounting
        programs
    Strong organizational and interpersonal skills

Education
    Blank University, Copeland, Texas
    Bachelor of Science in Accounting, GPA 4.0   May 23, 20–
    Capitol High School, Bent, Texas   20-- to 20–

Work Experience
    Prepared financial statements and performed   20-- to present
        other office duties for the Dean of the
        School of Business, Blank University
    French and Spanish tutor, Blank University
    Teacher at computer camp for children   20-- to 20--
        ages ten thru sixteen
    Part time bookkeeping and payroll, Seller's   20-- to 20--
        Insurance Company

"There are no obstacles that hard work and
preparation cannot cure."

Barbara Jordan

Miscellaneous

This is a collection of all those little things that you should know but that do not really fit into any category. It also gives me an opportunity to vent about some of my pet peeves.

Telephone

This should be so easy. We use the phone every day but not always correctly.

When You Phone

- Identify yourself.
- Do not hang up on answering machines, as caller ID will catch you in this nefarious deed.
- Leave a clear message with your phone number.
- Excuse yourself if you get a wrong number. Tell them what number you were attempting to call.
- Say "good-bye" and do not hang up until the other person does.

When You Receive a Call

In this day and age, people may be leery of identifying themselves when answering their phones. If you are uncomfortable about giving out any information, just say "hello."

❦ Take a thorough message.

❦ Do not shout to another room to inform someone he has a phone call.

❦ Say "good-bye" and hang up first.

Calling the Hearing or Speech Impaired

It is possible to telephone persons with speech or hearing impairments by using TTY relay services. You do not need to have any special equipment, but simply dial the toll free number listed in the front of your telephone book.

Answering Machines

Music and other extraneous messages (i.e., "Have a nice day!") should not be part of your message on the answering machine. Any of the following are appropriate.

❦ "You have reached the Vincent residence. Please leave your name and number and we will return your call as soon as possible." This message is appropriate for a single person (using "we") if she does not wish to advertise that she is living alone.

❦ "This is 667-4231. We are unable to answer the phone at this time. If you leave your name and number, we will return your call."

❦ "Please leave your name and phone number and we will return your call. Thank you." Although a bit ambiguous for the caller if they don't recognize your voice, you may use this if you would rather not give out your name or number.

Introductions

The Main Ideas

- Women are introduced to men.
- The older person is introduced to the younger.
- A president is introduced to a peon.
  Examples:

  > "Mrs. Blake, I'd like you to meet my friend, Cindy."
  > "Mr. President, this is John Jones, your new filing clerk."
  > "Melanie, have you met Justin Smith? Justin, this is Melanie Jones."

- Apologize if you forget a name.
- Correct it at once if your name is given incorrectly.
- If you are not introduced by someone else, introduce yourself. They have either forgotten one or more person's names or they are rude.
- It always helps if you add a sentence or two to the introduction that will encourage conversation.

  > "Jay, I'd like you to meet William Jones. William this is Jay Smith. He recently transferred here from Michigan and he loves to fly-fish. I thought you two might like to exchange some fishing stories."

Shaking Hands

It is appropriate to extend your hand to someone when introduced for the first time (except for royalty). It is perfectly acceptable for a woman to offer her hand first.

Use a firm grip, but do not be a crusher. We have a friend who always shakes my hand (when he can catch me) and it takes two days to recuperate from the pain he inflicts. I cannot believe he does not see me wincing.

Handshakes are also used to greet friends and as a farewell. Although in Texas you are just as likely to get a hug as a handshake.

Generally Speaking

Who's on First

- 🐝 Men should walk on the outside (street side) when walking with a woman.
- 🐝 Men precede women through a crowd, to the table in a restaurant (if there is no waitperson leading the way), to the dance floor, and up the stairs.
- 🐝 Women go first in church, the theater, or at a concert.
- 🐝 When walking down rows of seating, face the people you are trying to get by, rather than the stage.
- 🐝 When using elevators and doors in social situations be respectful of age and gender.

Hats

Men must take off their hats when they are indoors unless they are worn for religious reasons. This includes baseball caps, which may become a genetic mutation. They appear to be permanently attached to the heads of males between the ages of thirteen and thirty. This goes for cowboy hats, too. Take them off at concerts. People cannot see over your hat.

Seasonal Clothing

I can hardly believe I have to say this to anyone. Do not wear white shoes, pants, skirts, or suits before Memorial Day or after Labor

Day, unless you are a Good Humor man or a bride. I am sure there is a law about this somewhere, and I think violators should be arrested. (Athletic shoes are not included in the warning.)

Bumper Stickers

I cannot imagine why you would want one, but at least have the decency not to put profanity on the back of your car. My precocious daughter started reading when she was only two. I found it rather difficult to explain much of what she saw on the bumpers of automobiles.

Television

Never, never, never turn on the television when you are at a party. There is nothing more maddening than spending days preparing for a party only to have someone shut off your preprogrammed music to find a football score. Besides, you have no business messing with other peoples' sound systems.

Religion and Politics

Do not ask anyone what church they attend or what political party they belong to. If they initiate the conversation, fine, but otherwise it is none of your business.

Cell Phones and Beepers

Turn them off during parties, at the theater, and in restaurants unless you are a doctor.

Money

Do you know people who are constantly asking the cost of everything you buy? If you do not have the nerve to tell them how impolite they are, send me their number and I will call and tell them myself. If you are that interested in purchasing something, go price it for yourself.

Symphony

Never applaud at a symphony concert until the conductor has turned to face the audience or laid down his/her baton.

Gym Etiquette

With more and more people exercising on a regular basis, it seems that there are a growing number of complaints about behavior in the workout place.

- 🐾 Do not grunt and groan loudly while exercising.
- 🐾 If you sweat, clean up the equipment before you leave.
- 🐾 Do not hog the machines.
- 🐾 Always set the weights and equipment back to minimum levels.
- 🐾 Shower off before entering the whirlpool or steam room.
- 🐾 Put used towels in the appropriate container.
- 🐾 Do not borrow others' soap, shampoo, etc.
- 🐾 No skimpy outfits...men or women.

Flag Etiquette

Flags should be displayed from sunrise to sunset unless they are illuminated at night. No other flag should ever be displayed above the United States flag. If there is more than one flagstaff, the U.S. flag should be raised first and lowered last. On a dais, the flag should be above and behind the speaker with the blue (union) uppermost. If displayed from a staff at a meeting or church, it should be to the right of the speaker.

Texas Flag

If the Texas flag and the U.S. flag are flown from the same staff, the national flag should be on top. If they are flown from separate poles, the Texas flag is flown to the observer's left and at the same height as the national flag. The correct position for the Texas flag is white on top and red on the bottom.

The Texas Pledge of Allegiance

"Honor the Texas flag; I pledge allegiance to thee, Texas one and indivisible."

Ironically, under the terms of annexation to the United States in 1845, Texas retained the right to subdivide into four states.

Pledge of Allegiance and National Anthem of the United States

During the pledge of allegiance, all should stand, men should remove their hats, and all citizens of the United States should place their right hand over their heart. Military personnel should salute for the duration. This same behavior is appropriate for the singing of the national anthem, but women may stand with their hands at their sides. Nationals of other countries should rise and remain standing for both the pledge and anthem, but they do not need to participate.

Flags at Half-staff

Flags are flown at half-staff following the death of dignitaries. The flag should be raised to the top of the staff and then lowered to half-staff. It should be raised to the top again before being lowered completely at the end of the day. Flags should also be flown at half-staff on Memorial Day until noon.

National Flag Holidays

New Year's Day, Inauguration Day, Lincoln and Washington's Birthdays, Easter, Mother's Day, Armed Forces Day, Memorial Day, Flag Day, Independence Day, Labor Day, Constitution Day, Navy Day, Veterans Day, Thanksgiving, and Christmas.

Official State Holidays

- January 15, (celebrated the third Monday) Martin Luther King Day
- March 2, Texas Independence Day
- April 21, San Jacinto Day (battle for independence)
- June 19, Juneteenth (slaves informed in 1865 that they were free)
- August 27, Lyndon Johnson's Birthday

Calling Cards

Today calling cards are used mostly as gift enclosures. They should be printed (engraving is preferred) on heavy ecru or white card stock.

Men

Men's cards should measure 3⅜" x 1½" or 3½" x 2". Your title as well as junior or senior may be abbreviated.

Mr. Raymond Thomas Hill, Jr.

Single Woman

Their cards should measure 2⅞" x 2". No title precedes your full name.

Susan Lee Manchester

Married Woman

The card measures 3⅛" x 2¼". The title Mrs. is followed by her husband's name. Doctors use Dr. followed by their name.

Mrs. Raymond Thomas Hill, Jr.

Dr. Roberta Collins Hill

Couples

The card should measure 3⅜" x 2½". Mrs. is always used on social cards, even if the woman has another professional title.

Mr. and Mrs. Raymond Thomas Hill, Jr.

Holiday Cards

Christmas cards should always be signed, even if they are imprinted with your name.

Names   Margie and Mike Green
Ellie, Cory, and Bess

Margie, Mike, Ellie
Cory and Bess Green

The Green Family

Your return address should be included on all greeting cards. The post office prefers it on the front left-hand top of the envelope (because it is easier for them to write return to sender and circle the address), but the return address should be handwritten or embossed on the envelope flap. It should contain the address but not the name of the sender.

Holiday cards are the *only* type of correspondence on which you may sign another person's name along with yours. The signer's name should be written last.

Holiday Letters

When I was a child we always received one or two holiday letters, and my mother hated them. The children were all geniuses, and the family had spent six months in Europe. She called them brag notes. I personally love to receive these letters. It gives me a chance to catch up with old friends. I take delight in the fact that they want to share their family news with me. I still correspond with my high school civics teacher, as well as my children's teachers and various cousins that I have not seen in years. While I would love to have the time to write each a personal note, I find the holiday letter fills the gap, and I try to add a personal note on each letter.

Photo Greeting Cards

Well, if I like the holiday letter, you could guess I love receiving the photo greetings. You do need to remember to sign these personally, even if they are imprinted.

Sending Holiday Cards to Non-Christians

If you wish to send holiday greetings to non-Christians, you should select a card that states "Seasons Greetings" or "Holiday Wishes."

Business Holiday Cards

Holiday cards sent to business associates should be generic in nature, similar to those for non-Christians. Your spouse's name should not appear on the card unless he/she is a business or personal acquaintance of the associate.

Kwanzaa

Kwanzaa was started in the United States in 1966. It is a celebration of African-American culture honoring the traditions of African ancestors. It lasts for seven days and begins on December 26. A table is set with a straw mat. A candle holder (kinara) holds one black candle representing unity, three red candles representing purpose, creativity, and faith, followed by three green candles representing self-determination, collective work, and cooperative economics.

A candle is lit each day. Fruit and vegetables, as well as an ear of corn representing each child in the house, are displayed. The celebration culminates in a feast held on December 31. Gifts, usually handmade or dealing with African art or culture, are given on January 1.

Hanukkah

Hanukkah is the celebration of Jewish recovery of their Holy Temple from the Greeks and commemorates a miracle that occurred. There was only enough oil left to light the menorah for one day. Miraculously, the oil burned for eight full days, until the supply could be replenished.

Hanukkah is celebrated for eight days. Each day a candle is lit on a menorah called a hanukkiyah. A four-sided top called a dreidel is associated with the holiday because during the time the Greeks took over the Temple, the teaching of the Torah was outlawed. Children would gather to study the Torah secretly and would pretend they were playing with a dreidel when the soldiers neared.

Speaking Plainly

Although the soft sound of a Southern drawl is music to my ears, those melodious tones are often interrupted by the jarring sound of mispronounced words and grammatical errors that creep into the vernacular. Sometimes Texans are so relaxed, they just drop the endings from words or slur the beginnings. While this may be charming in speech, it plays havoc with our written language. The only appropriate place for words with dropped "g's" on the end is in country and western music: lovin', leavin', lyin', cryin', and dyin'.

"Futhuh"

<u>Farther</u> measures distance. "It is farther from Houston to Dallas than from Houston to Waco."
<u>Further</u> measures time or amount. "We need further time to study your plan."
<u>Father</u> is a male parent. "He is the father of my children."

Leave and Let

<u>Leave</u> means to depart. "I will leave for Austin at noon."
<u>Let</u> means to allow or permit. "I will let you have five dollars."

Fixin' to

Either you are <u>about to do something</u> or you are <u>getting ready to do something</u>, not fixin' to do something.

Y'all

Y'all is perfectly okay to use, but it is not supposed to be used singularly.

Than and From

You are never different than someone, you are <u>different from</u> someone.
She is different from her twin sister.

Verbs and Adverbs

A verb is a word that indicates action or a state of being. An adverb "describes" a verb and usually ends in "ly."
"I swim slowly." Slowly tells <u>how</u> I swim.

Nouns and Adjectives

A noun is the name of a person, place, or thing. An adjective
"describes" a noun.
"I am a slow swimmer." Slow tells <u>what kind</u> of swimmer I am.

Modifiers

You would not say, "I am a slowly swimmer" or "I swim slow."

Good and Well

<u>Good</u> is an adjective. "You have good posture." Good describes
your posture.
<u>Well as an adjective</u>. "I am not well." Well describes your health.
<u>Well as an adverb</u>. "You type well." Well describes your ability to
type.

Can and May

<u>Can</u> indicates that you are able to do something.
"You can lift one hundred pounds."
<u>May</u> indicates that you have permission to do something or that it
is possible.
"You may go to town."
"It may be true."

On Account of . . .

Use the phrase "due to" or the word "because" instead.

Set/Sit

<u>Set</u> means to place. "Set this down on the table."
<u>Sit</u> means to rest or be seated. "Sit down and eat."

Try And...

Use "try to" instead.   "Try to attend the dance."

Teach and Learn

Teach means to impart knowledge. "Teach me to read."
Learn means to gain knowledge. "I will learn to read."

Between and Among

Between means there are two people. "She divided the candy
   between the two sisters."
Among indicates more than two people. "The teacher walked
   among her students."

Possessive Pronouns

Your (your hat)
"Your hat is on the table."
Its (its property)
"The city sold its property."
Their (their commission)
"Their commission was
fifty percent."
Theirs (theirs is broken)
"My bicycle works, but
theirs is broken."
Whose (whose hat)
"Whose hat is that?"

Contractions

You're (you are)
"You're the new president."
It's (it is)
"It's time to go."
They're (they are)
"They're going to California."

There's (there is)
"There's a robin in that tree."

Who's (who is)
"Who's the best swimmer?"

Who/Whom

If you can substitute I, she, he, we, or they in the sentence, use
   who.
   "Who will take us to the dance?" She will take us to the dance.

If you can substitute me, her, him, us, or them in the sentence, use <u>whom</u>.
"I need someone whom I can talk to." I can talk to <u>her</u>.

I, You, He, She, We, They

Use these pronouns when it is the <u>subject of the verb</u>.
"Susan and I will shop."
"They may eat dinner now."
"We might fly to Austin."
Use these pronouns when the pronoun occurs <u>after the "to be" verb</u> (am, is, was, were) or <u>in a verbal phrase</u>.
"Was it she who played the piano?"
It was <u>she</u> who played the piano.

Me, Us, Him, Her, Them

Use these pronouns when the pronoun is the <u>direct or indirect object of a verb</u>.
"The cookies are for you and him" The cookies are for <u>him</u>.

Free

You get things <u>free</u>, not <u>for free</u>. "The hats were free with a purchase of ten gallons of gas."

Alumna, Alumnus

The <u>female</u> term is alumna; the plural version is alumnae.
The <u>male</u> term is alumnus; the plural version is alumni.

Exact Same

Use either word separately, but do not use them together. They mean the same thing.

Words Often Pronounced Incorrectly

ask	not aks
library	not liberry
Massachusetts	not Massatoosits
similar	not simular
et cetera	not excetera
athlete	not athaleet
Realtor	not reelitor
salmon	not sallmen (the "l" is silent)
accessory	not assessory ("cc" is pronounced ak)
escape	not excape
supposedly	not supposably
nuclear	not nucular
Bermuda	not Bamooda

"No one has a finer command of the language than the person who keeps his mouth shut."

Sam Rayburn

Dining

Sharing a wonderful meal with someone whose company you enjoy can be a great experience. Many things contribute to the overall feeling of pleasure, including the service, the atmosphere, and the food. Stress, however, can ruin a social occasion. The basics of dining etiquette are easy to remember. If you practice them at home, you will be prepared when it really matters.

Place Cards

Place cards are made of thick ecru or white stock and come in a variety of styles. Black ink should be used for formal dinners. Names include a title, first name, and surname: Mrs. Robert Alexander. (Note: women use their husband's name, even widows, unless they are divorced, then they are Mrs. Elizabeth Alexander.) Set cards just above the dessert utensils and centered over the dinner plate.

- Use place cards for groups of eight people or more.
- If you are attending a dinner at a home, restaurant, or charity event, *do not* move the place cards. Your hostess has arranged the guests in some sort of pattern, according to her wishes, and it would be unspeakably rude to tamper with her decision. The same goes for charity events. Tables are usually assigned based on the donation level. If you do not like where you are sitting, ante up a little more money next year.

🍷 Table listings are used to direct guests to their seats. Cards, with numbers at the top and the names of the guests seated at the table, are displayed in an area adjacent to the party or reception. Individually addressed envelopes containing seating placements may also be used.

🍷 Introduce yourself to others at your table.

Coats

At a restaurant, men should check their coats. Women take theirs to the table and place them over the back of their chair. At galas and private parties, all coats may be checked.

Seating

The place of honor is to the right of the hostess. Husbands and wives should not be seated next to each other.

Approaching and Departing the Table

🍷 The person who shows you to your table in a restaurant should pull out the chair and assist the female guest. If the waiter does not make a move to do so, the male should assist her.

🍷 If there are two women to seat, help the one the waiter is not helping. Men should enter their chair from the left side. If two or more women are unescorted, then they seat themselves.

🍷 In business situations, women seat themselves.

🌿 You should not leave the table during the meal unless it is an emergency. If a female leaves, all the men at the table should stand on her exit and return. The closest male should help with her chair.

🌿 When leaving the table following the meal, the man should stand and help the woman exit her chair on the right, then push both chairs in to the table.

The Pristine Table

You have heard that elbows do not belong on the table, but actually it is permissible to let your elbows touch the table as long as you are not using them as spindles to support your body. Rocking back in forth in your chair, however, is not allowed.

At a dinner in a private home, do not take your cocktails to the dining table. Nothing should be put on the table that is not part of the centerpiece or meal. No papers, purses, or sunglasses are allowed. Your purse, evening bag, or briefcase should be placed on the floor by your right foot.

Tablecloths

Invariably tablecloths get creases from being laundered and folded. They should be ironed before being placed on the table. To achieve a good finish on linens, spray starch them. Allow the starch to soak in for thirty seconds before ironing.

Only one lengthwise center fold on the cloth is proper. If using two tablecloths in tandem, the center creases should be matched. The cloth should hang eight to ten inches below the edge of the table and clear the chair seat. Semiformal length is a twelve- to fifteen-inch drop, formal is an eighteen-inch drop, and the buffet table should be draped to the floor.

Tablecloth Sizes

Table shape	Actual measurement	Cloth size	Number of people seated
Round	36" - 44"	60"	4
	44" - 54"	70"	4-6
	60" - 70"	90"	6-8
Square	28" x 28" - 40" x 40"	52" x 52"	4
Rectangle	28" x 46" - 36" x 54"	52" x 70"	4-6
	36" x 56" - 42" x 64"	60" x 84"	6-8
	42" x 72" - 42" x 84"	60" x 102"	8-10
Oval	42" x 90" - 42" x 96"	60" x 120"	10-12
	42" x 100" - 42" x 120"	60" x 142"	12-16

Monograms

Square linens are monogrammed in a corner, and rectangular linens are monogrammed in the center of each long side.

Protector Mats

Many companies that make custom protector mats for your dining table advertise in the back of magazines. They will send you instructions for measuring your table with and without leaves. These mats protect your table from heat and spills and can be easily folded for storage.

Napkins

If you are in a formal restaurant, the waiter will place your napkin in your lap when you are seated. Otherwise, put your napkin in your lap as soon as your host takes his. A dinner napkin should remain folded in half, with the fold toward your waist. Luncheon size napkins should be fully opened before placing in your lap. If you drop your napkin on the floor, leave it there and tell your waiter you need another. Of course, if you are dining at Bennie's Hash House, you had better retrieve it before someone steps on it.

Napkins should be used to dab your lips, not scrub your face. You should blot off any excess lipstick before coming to the table …no red lip marks on the napkin. *Never* use your napkin as a handkerchief or as a repository for an inedible chunk of food.

The end of the meal is signaled when the host places his napkin on the table. When the meal is completed, lay your napkin on the table next to the *left* side of your plate. However, at a formal dinner, the napkin should be placed to the *right* side following the meal. Do not refold, spindle, or mutilate it. If you must leave the table during a meal, place your napkin on your chair.

Sizes

The standard sizes for napkins are ten, thirteen, seventeen, or twenty inch squares. Napkins are monogrammed in the center or in a corner.

Napkin Presentation

Napkins may be placed to the left of your fork, on the dinner plate, or in the water glass.

Napkin Folding

Napkins may be folded in numerous fashions, but here are a few simple ideas.

Fold the napkin in half to form a rectangle with the folded edge at the bottom.

Fold the top of the first layer down two inches then fold again two inches.

Turn the napkin over and bring the right edge to the center and
  fold over, then fold over itself again. Your silverware will fit in
  the pocket.

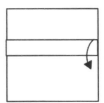 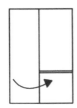 

Fold all four corners to the center. Fold new corners to the center.
Turn the napkin over and fold the four corners to the center.
Pull up the loose points under each corner and pull outward. A
  flower shape will form.

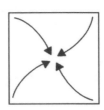

Fold the napkin to form a triangle, then fold left and right points
  to the bottom.
Hold the points and turn the napkin over and put the points at the
  top.
Raise the bottom point to meet the top point.
Lift the napkin at the bottom center so that the napkin stands up.

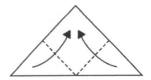 

Removing Stains From Linens

The faster you get to a stain, the better chance you have of removing it. Do not machine wash until you have pretreated the stain. Never put a stained item in the dryer or iron it. Heat can set stains. Sometimes a stain will surface after the linens have dried, so it is best to air-dry them to make sure the stain is really gone. No removal technique is guaranteed to remove all stains, and each fabric reacts differently to cleaners. Use the following suggestions with caution.

Red wine

Put salt on the stain, gently rub and rinse with cool water, then wash. If the stain has dried, treat with club soda, then wash. Linens can also be pretreated with a color-safe bleach.

White wine

Clean the stain with a solution of white vinegar and water, then rinse and wash.

Mildew and Scorch Marks

These marks are not always removable, but you can try liquid bleach in hot water.

Lipstick

Pretreat with a stain remover and use rubbing alcohol to remove any remaining stain. Rinse and wash.

Chocolate

Soak in cold water for half an hour. Then use a stain remover or a paste of cornstarch and water, let dry, and then brush off. Rinse and wash.

Grease

Pretreat with a stain remover and wash.

Coffee and Tea

Pretreat the stain and wash immediately with detergent and bleach.

Carpet Stains

Read this before you do anything. I ruined my carpet trying to clean a tea stain with a commercial cleaner. Even a professional could not remove the stain after I "set" it with an over-the-counter product. Call your rug cleaning professional for advice.

Save an extra piece of your carpet to stain and test treat.

Clean the stain as quickly as possible. Blot up any liquids or scoop up any solid materials. Apply cleaner to cloth rather than to the spot, and work from the outside of the spot inward. If you plan to tackle the stain yourself, you could try one of these procedures:

Coffee, Tea, and Pet Stains

These can be cleaned with a teaspoon of mild laundry detergent and two cups of water. Put the solution on a clean cloth and work it into the carpet. Rinse with tepid water and blot with a clean towel. Repeat steps until stain is gone. Then place clean paper towels over the area and weight them with a colorfast object. Change towels until all the water is absorbed. If the stain does not come out, try equal parts of water and vinegar using the process above and absorb the dampness with paper towels.

Butter, Ink, and Lipstick

These need to be removed with a dry cleaning fluid.

Wine, Chocolate, and General Food Stains

These can be cleaned with a solution of one teaspoon of mild laundry detergent and two cups of water. Apply with a clean cloth and work into the stain. Rinse and blot. If the stain remains, mix one tablespoon household ammonia (nonbleaching and nonsudsing) with one cup tepid water. Apply with a clean cloth and work into stain. Rinse and blot thoroughly. Then neutralize the ammonia solution with equal parts vinegar and water, blotting and rinsing. Then place paper towels over the area and weight them with a colorfast object. Change paper towels until dry.

Table Decorations

Candle wicks should be charred before using. Place candles above or below eye level and light only after dark. **Centerpieces**, as well as candles, should not obstruct the view of anyone at the table. I have been to many charity events where people pulled the centerpieces off the table because they could not converse with each other. Sit at the table and determine the proper height of the arrangement before you talk to your florist or order flowers.

To prolong the life of your **flower arrangements**, use the floral preservative that is delivered with the arrangement. Mix it with the prescribed amount of water and add some of it each day to maintain the water level in the arrangement.

Keep your arrangement away from heat, air-conditioning, and sunlight. Store it in a cool place when not displayed.

If you are arranging your own flowers, trim off all the leaves that will be below the water line and cut the stems to length while they are submerged in water. If you do not have preservative, a little sugar water will work and a drop of hydrogen peroxide will keep the water from getting a rancid odor.

Flatware

Flatware refers to eating utensils. Stainless steel, silverplate, and sterling silver are all types of flatware. There are two sizes available: the luncheon or dinner. The dinner size has a slightly larger knife and fork and is usually priced higher than the luncheon. Flatware is placed one inch from the edge of the table.

Silverware may be *monogrammed* as follows:

🌑 Before marriage, use a single monogram of your surname.

H

🌑 For wedding silver for Karen Melinda Henry and Mark Henry Bower. (Using the bride's maiden initials.)

K$_H$M or **KMH**

(More commonly, using her first two initials and her new last initial.)

KMB or **B**

🌑 Never use the groom's monogram except on personal items for him.

Flatware and Dining

🌑 When dining, start with the utensils farthest away from your plate and work your way in.

🌑 If a piece of your silverware drops to the floor, do not retrieve it; ask for another.

❦ Do not put used silverware back on the table. It should always rest on the dish from which you are eating.

❦ At the end of the meal, your knife and fork should be placed at an angle across your plate (about ten and four on the clock), with the knife at the top with the blade facing you and the fork below with tines facing up or down.

❦ Do not leave utensils in a cup, glass, or a non-flat dish. Remove utensils from a bowl or cup and set on the plate below.

❦ If you are merely pausing in your dining, your knife and fork should be slightly crossed at the center of the plate.

❦ Do not gesture with your utensils.

Caring for Your Flatware

Stainless may be washed in the dishwasher, but do not use lemon detergents. It is not a good idea to mix metals in the dishwasher. Aluminum and silver should not be washed with stainless. If hand washing, utensils should not be left to soak.

Silverplate should not be cleaned in the dishwasher. All the precautions used with stainless should also be observed with silverplate. Eggs and acid foods should be rinsed immediately. Avoid cleaning dips as well as the metal sheets and soda washes. Cleaning directions for silverplate are the same as for sterling silver.

Sterling silver should always be hand washed and dried immediately. All the same precautions that apply to stainless and silverplate should be observed.

Cleaning and Storing

Silver and silverplate should be cleaned with a product like Tarnish Shield by 3M™. Apply with a clean sponge and keep rinsing the sponge to keep it clean. Rinse the object in hot water and dry immediately. Handle with cotton gloves to avoid fingerprints. If there are parts of a silver or silverplated object that should not be exposed to moisture, such as wood handles, felt pads, or linings, use a polish that is rubbed on and buffed off with a clean cloth. (Goddard's™ Long Shine Silver Polish)

Any rubber (latex) product (like gloves) should not be used with silver. Nitrile gloves work well for polishing silver. For weekly cleanings, a treated flannel polishing cloth keeps tarnish under control. Polishing cloth and silvercloth are available from Nancy's Notions® online or mail order.

Wrap clean silver in acid free tissue or Silvershield™ Silvercloth. Anti-tarnish strips will help retard the tarnishing process, and silica gel will help reduce humidity. The anti-tarnish strips have varying shelf lives, so be sure to replace them as needed.

Glasses or Crystal

The difference between glass and crystal is that crystal is better quality and may be hand blown or hand cut. Goblets are for water or iced tea. There are also special iced tea glasses that are shaped like a goblet, but with a deeper bowl. Champagne may either be served in tall thin flutes or in the wider champagne/sherbets. Wine may be served in a variety of glasses, but as a rule, white wine goes in the one with the smaller bowl, red in the larger, as it needs more room to "breathe."

The wine glass for the main course should be positioned directly above the tip of the dinner knife. This is called the guide glass. Glasses used prior to the meal will be placed in front of this glass and those used following the meal will be placed behind. Glasses will be in an angled line.

❧ Red wine and water goblets should be held by the base of the bowl.

❧ Goblets and flutes containing chilled wine are held by the stem to keep from warming the wine.

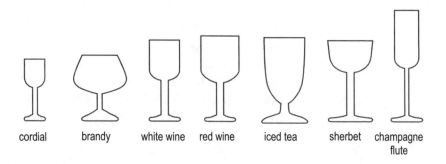

cordial   brandy   white wine   red wine   iced tea   sherbet   champagne flute

💚 Never "clink" glasses when making a toast. Merely raise your glass and tip it towards the person being toasted.

💚 Never look over the top of your glass when drinking.

Table Settings

When dining, start with the utensils farthest away from your plate and work your way in.

The napkin may be placed on your plate, to the left of the forks, or in the water glass. (See Napkins.) The butter knife on the bread and butter plate points to the left. The blades on the other knives face the plate.

A formal dinner presentation would look similar to the following:

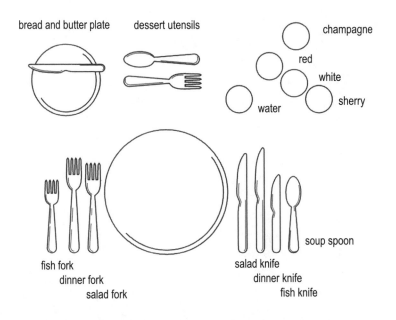

bread and butter plate   dessert utensils   champagne

red

white

sherry

water

fish fork
dinner fork
salad fork

salad knife
dinner knife
fish knife

soup spoon

Casual setting:

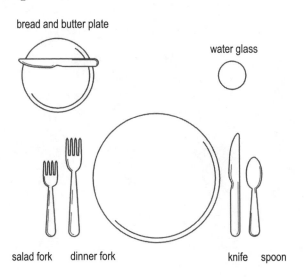

bread and butter plate

water glass

salad fork   dinner fork   knife   spoon

Menu Cards

Menu cards usually measure five by seven inches and are printed on heavy ecru or white paper that supports its own weight. Each course is listed, as well as accompanying wines. Sometimes they are displayed on decorative stands, but they may be placed to the left of the forks or rested against a goblet. Everyone may have his or her own card, or they may be placed strategically around the table so that all can view them. Although they are not required, they add an elegant touch to the table setting and allow the guests to pace their dining.

Sample menu card:

(Event or Organization name and date may appear here)

Crab Bisque

Baby Greens with Raspberry Vinaigrette

Veal Cordon Bleu
Potatoes Gratin
Petite Pois

Chocolate Ambrosia

(wines may be listed here)

Smoking

Do not ask if you may smoke in someone's home unless you see ashtrays set out. This includes cigarettes, cigars, or pipes. Even if you are seated in the smoking section of a restaurant, you should not smoke between courses—only before you begin your meal or after your meal is completed.

Ordering Dinner

We all know that women have learned to read, can speak, and are capable of ordering a meal for themselves. Nevertheless, I actually liked it when my husband would take my order and give it to the waitperson. He just quit doing it because it seemed to confuse the waiter too much.

Your waiter should take the orders from all the women first and then the men. Do not count on it. If the waiter asks the man first, he should turn to his date and say, "Jane, what would you like?" It's a nice way to do things correctly, even if the waiter does not.

Entree (pronounced "on tray") really means the dish served before the main course, but it is used in most U.S. restaurants to signify the main course. Sometimes, if the restaurant serves elaborate desserts, you will need to state a dessert preference when you order your meal.

Hors d'oeuvres and Crudités

Hor d'oeuvres (pronounced "or dervs") can refer to a light course of food preceding the main entree, including items such as soup, shrimp, or small servings of food. It can also refer to a variety of finger foods served at a buffet style party. Crudités (pronounced "crew de tays") usually refer to bite-size pieces of vegetables.

If your host has suggested "something to start with..." order the hor d'oeuvre of your choice. If you have no clue as to what the rest of the group will do, order something small like a cup of soup. Soup does not take long to prepare or consume in the event that no one else orders an hors d'oeuvre.

Serving

Food should be served from the left and beverages served from the right. Plates are removed from the right side.

Significant Others

🌱 When dining at a private home, wait for the hostess to begin eating. In a restaurant, begin when all at your table have been served.

🌱 At a large event, begin when your table has been served. If the meal is buffet, you may begin when you and your escort return to the table.

🌱 Spoon soup away from you and sip off the edge of the spoon.

🌱 Bread should be broken, not cut, into bite-size pieces and buttered just before eating. Hot rolls may be opened and buttered.

🌱 Salt and pepper should be passed together. Always taste your food before seasoning. All food and condiments should be passed to your right. Point the handle of a serving dish or pitcher toward the receiver.

- At the end of a formal meal a small bowl (finger bowl) with a slice of lemon in it may be placed before you. Dip your fingers gently and dry them on your napkin.

- Sorbet (pronounced "sore bay") is often served between the fish and meat courses to cleanse the palate. It is not dessert.

- Never blow your nose or pick your teeth at the table. Keep your hands away from your face.

- If you bite into something that is not chewable, remove it with your fingers and hide it under something on your plate. Do not spit it into your napkin.

- Salad should be cut with a fork, with the exception of iceberg lettuce, which may be cut with a knife.

- It is okay to ask for a doggie bag at a restaurant, but not at a party.

- You may put on lipstick at the table, but nothing else in the way of makeup.

Things You May Eat With Your Fingers

Vegetables: corn on the cob (do not butter all at once), artichokes, and asparagus (no sauce)

Fast food: hamburgers, fries, tacos, fried chicken, pizza

Cocktail buffet food: sandwiches, cookies, and grapes or berries with stems on

Dining in French

Many restaurants and clubs will have menu items written in French. Do not panic. You already are accustomed to many French food terms like quiche, croissant, and canapé. If you cannot pronounce something, point to it on the menu and ask the waiter for the correct pronunciation. Do not be intimidated. I've had many a waitperson pronounce the word "salmon" incorrectly. It seems they feel the "l" should not be silent.

Cooking Methods

à la – in the style of
au jus – in its own juice
au lait – with milk
en croûte – baked in a crust
au gratin – baked dish, usually with cheese
meunière – lightly floured and sautéed in butter

Sauces

bernaise sauce – sauce made with herbs, white wine, butter, and egg yolks
béchamel sauce – white sauce
beurre blanc – butter sauce
beurre noir – browned butter sauce
bordelaise sauce – brown sauce made with wine
hollandaise sauce – made with egg yolks, butter, lemon, and tarragon
mornay sauce – white sauce with cheese

Vegetables

asperges – asparagus
courgette – zucchini
champignons – mushrooms
haricots vertes – green beans
pois – peas

Fruits

cerise – cherry
fraise – strawberry
pomme – apple
pamplemousse – grapefruit
pêche – peach
poire – pear

Fish

poisson – fish
crevettes – shrimp
huîtres – oysters
homard – lobster
palourdes – clams

Meat

boeuf – beef
chateaubriand – steak
tournedos – beef fillet
canard – duck
coq au vin – chicken in wine sauce
carré d'agneau – rack of lamb
foie gras – duck and goose liver
jambon – ham
lapin – rabbit
porc – pork
poulet – chicken

Courses for a Formal Dinner

During a formal dinner, the entire meal is served by hired help. Food is never offered for a second helping, and butter is not served with bread.

First course – hors d'eouvres
Second course – soup
Third course – fish
Fourth course – entreé
Fifth course – meat, potatoes, vegetable, the main course
Sixth course – salad
Seventh course – dessert, followed by the presentation of
    finger bowls

"It's okay to eat with your fingers...the food is clean."

Anonymous

Y'all Come Back Now, Ya' Hear?

I love to cook and entertain. I have edited two cookbooks and catered a charity event for one hundred twenty-five people. Like most Texans, I am instilled with a large dose of Southern hospitality. I am at my happiest when my home is filled with my friends.

If you shy away from entertaining, start out simply. Have a few friends over for a cookout. Don't overextend your cooking skills. Plan ahead. Schedule shopping, cleaning, and decorating time as well as personal time for yourself.

Guest List

When entertaining, you first need to decide how many guests you wish to include and how many guests you can comfortably fit into your entertaining space. I happen to like the "feel" of fifty people in my house. They can move about freely, but it does not feel too crowded if they congregate in one area, which they inevitably do. I have tried putting food and drink in various places, but they all still pack into the living room. If you want them to make use of your outdoor space, you need to put something really great on the patio to motivate them to move outside.

Hiring a Caterer

Check any caterer's references and find out the amount of the deposit (usually 1/4), when it is due, and what the cancellation policy is. What services do they provide? Are linens, waiters, bartenders, and servers included? Do they decorate the tables? How will they serve the food? What about providing dishes, glasses, and silverware? Is the cleanup and setup included? Will there be additional taxes and gratuities? Ascertain what menu options are available, when the head count is due, and what margin they allow for unexpected guests. Finally, will they leave the leftover food and beverages for you, and are they willing to pack them up?

Most importantly, *taste their food*. Be sure to specify brands of liquor if they are supplying it. The average cost of a catered dinner is $35-$50 per person, not including drinks.

Self-Catered

❦ If you plan to cook some of the food for your party, discuss this option with the caterer. Make sure he or she is willing to heat and serve your food.

❦ If you are preparing all the food yourself, make the items as far ahead as possible and freeze them in disposable pans.

❦ Meats may be grilled for a few minutes to give them a charcoal flavor and then finished in the oven.

❦ Prepare the most perishable items last.

❦ Label all pans with the thawing instructions and the cooking temperatures. Allow ample time for items to thaw in the refrigerator.

❦ Mark serving trays and utensils for each particular food.

🌶 Have your help arrive an hour and a half before the start of your party. They will have time to heat all the food and set the tables.

Estimating Food Amounts

Caterers will usually tell you that they allow five to ten bites of pick-up food per person, depending on the type of party. It will vary with the time of day and just how hungry the crowd is. Having extra food is always better than running out of food.

Here are some guidelines from the USDA handbook "Food for Institutions," for the average food consumption.

Beef (boneless)	¼-½ lb. per person
Chicken	13 lbs. per 25 people
Salad	one cup per person
Black-eyed peas	½ cup per person (Texas caviar)
Potatoes	4½ quarts per 25 people
Baked beans	¾ gallon per 25 people
Hamburger	9 lbs. per 25 people
Hot dogs	6½ lbs. per 25 people
Ice cream	32 (½ c. servings) per gallon

Coffee

Coffee made from Arabica beans is the finest. Because coffee is perishable, grind your beans just before using them. You may freeze coffee beans in airtight containers to maintain their freshness.

🌶 Clean your coffee maker and use a stainless steel, gold mesh, or glass filter.

- ❦ Unless you like the way your tap water tastes, use bottled water. Use cold not hot water.

- ❦ Spread the grounds evenly in the filter and always brew a full pot. The standard measure is two level teaspoons per 3/4 cup of water. Three teaspoons may be used if you like stronger coffee.

- ❦ Remove the basket just before brewing is finished, as the last bit of coffee brewed is bitter.

- ❦ Place your brewed coffee in a thermal carafe as soon as brewing is complete. Preheat your carafe with hot water, and your coffee will remain hot for up to two hours.

- ❦ Allow two to three cups per person.

Tea

Tea Types

There are over 1,500 varieties of tea grown worldwide. The major tea classifications are:

Black teas, which include Darjeeling, Earl Grey, and English breakfast, have been exposed to air to allow the leaves to change color in a process called oxidation.

Green teas, like Sencha and Lung Ching, are made when the tea leaves just wither naturally.

Oolong teas are made with a combination of black and green leaves and include Silvertip, Oolong, and Black Dragon.

White tea, which is made in China, is very rare.

Herbal teas are made from herbs rather than tea leaves. They have gained in popularity over the years because they contain no caffeine, and they are also available in many delicious flavors.

Preparing Hot Tea

Loose tea provides better flavor than a tea bag and will remain fresh for about one year if stored in an airtight container. Allow one teaspoon per six-ounce cup. Heat your water until just boiling and pour over the leaves. You may make tea by the cup or by the pot. There are tea infusers that will hold the leaves inside a perforated container so that your tea can brew without getting loose leaves in your cup. Teapots may also have infusers. If your teapot does not have an infuser, then you will need to use a tea strainer when you are pouring your tea into the cups.

Cover the pot with a lid, or cover your cup with a saucer while the tea steeps. Never let your tea steep for more than five minutes. Three minutes is the maximum for some types of tea. If you are using tea bags, do not steep them as long, and squeeze the bag with tea tongs before you discard them.

Sun Tea

The sun tea fad started in the seventies and still has fans today. The basic recipe for twelve servings is:

Use cold water to fill a two-quart container and add two-thirds cup of loose tea leaves. Set in the sun for four hours or leave out on the counter overnight. Strain and serve over ice.

Iced Tea Concentrate for a Group

For thirty glasses of iced tea, take 1½ quarts of boiling water and add 1⅓ cup of loose tea. Cover and steep for four minutes and strain. Refrigerate after cooling.

Servings: For each ten glasses of tea, mix one cup of the concentrate with 1½ quarts of boiling water. Serve over ice.

For larger amounts use the following:

30 glasses	use 8 ounces of concentrate and 1½ gallons of water
100 glasses	use 32 ounces of concentrate and 6 gallons of water

Old-fashioned Iced Tea

8-10 servings	1 quart boiling water	⅓ cup loose tea or 15 tea bags
25 servings	1½ gallons boiling water	¾ cup loose tea
100 servings	6 gallons boiling water	3¼ cups loose tea

Cover the tea leaves with boiling water and let stand for five minutes. Strain and cool before refrigerating or the tea will turn cloudy.

Afternoon Tea

Afternoon tea is a fairly formal affair consisting of small finger sandwiches and desserts such as cookies, muffins, scones, and fruit tarts. The serving of the tea is the major focus, and being asked to "pour" is considered an honor. All guests should be seated during the tea. Accompaniments to the tea include sugar, lemon, and warm milk. Hot water to dilute the tea should also be available. Milk, if desired, should be poured in the cup before the tea. Allow two to three cups of tea per person or three to four cups of punch (if serving) per person.

Tea Sandwiches

Sandwiches may be made on any flavor bread, including sweet fruit breads. Remove all the crusts and cut a loaf of bread into quarter-inch-thick slices. Use two tablespoons of the desired filling per slice. You may top them with another slice of bread or leave them open-faced. Cut into thirds. If you desire, you may use cookie cutters to make different shaped sandwiches or bake shaped breads. Some suggested fillings are flavored cream cheese, cucumber and watercress, or smoked salmon.

High Tea

Somehow we have confused the term "high tea" and have assumed it was a step up in formality from afternoon tea. High tea originated in Britain by the working class, when they paused to have a cross between afternoon tea and supper. It is usually served between three and four o'clock. The fare is hardier than afternoon tea and includes meat and fish dishes as well as heavier desserts.

Peppers

Having been born "North of Oklahoma," I did not have the luxury of acclimating my palate to the chile pepper. The reason everyone else I know can eat copious amounts of *hot* food is that their bodies have developed a tolerance to peppers and so they crave hotter and hotter food. My eyes are watering, and my friends are still eating.

Pepper is a term for a family of plants, while chile pepper is a generic term for the hotter peppers in the family. (The plural is chiles.) Chiles are hot because of a substance called capsaicin that is found on the ribs of the pepper and the seeds. Always wear plastic gloves and eye protection when seeding and preparing chiles.

Capsaicin acts on the pain receptors in the mouth. It is soluble in alcohol, but not in water. Consuming yogurt or sour cream eases the pain because they both contain the protein casein, which breaks down the bond of capsaicin to your mouth.

The heat of the chile is measured in Scoville units. Here are the Scoville ratings of a few popular peppers:

bell	0
cherry	100-500
jalapeno	2,500
cayenne	30,000
habanero	100,000-350,000

red savina habanero	577,000 (the hottest pepper ever tested)

Do not confuse chiles with the meat dish flavored with red chili peppers, chili, which originated in Texas.

"Even if your enemy passes your way, you must feed him before you shoot him."

O. Henry

Alcoholic Beverages

In spite of the fact that Texas is considered part of the Bible Belt, there are equal numbers of Catholics and Baptists in the state. Out of 254 counties, only 53 are "dry." Alcohol, in all probability, will be a part of most social events.

Do not order an alcoholic beverage unless your host suggests a drink or wine before dinner. If you order first and your host does not order a drink, do not order a refill. If you are at a party or banquet and wine glasses are already set on the table, but you do not wish to partake, when the server comes, gently place two fingers over the top of the wine glass indicating that you do not want any wine. Do not turn your glass over.

Stocking Your Bar

Those who know me well are probably laughing out loud. I am sure I have not consumed a liter of alcohol in my entire lifetime, and I am telling you how to stock your bar. Well, stop laughing. I entertain a lot and I have done lots of research.

- The well-stocked bar should contain at least a one-liter bottle of the following: bourbon, gin, light rum, dark rum, scotch, tequila, vermouth (sweet and dry), vodka, and red and white wine.

- Additional items include brandy, port, sherry, and a variety of liqueurs.

❧ Mixers: tonic water, club soda, mineral water and sodas, as well as mixes for margaritas, etc.

❧ Fruit and vegetable juices, coconut milk, grenadine, and garnishes such as lemons, limes, olives, cocktail onions, maraschino cherries, coarse salt, and mint leaves.

❧ Do not forget extra ice.

Okay, now you have stocked the bar, but how much will everyone drink?

Servings Per Bottle

❧ A liter bottle, which is about 34 ounces, will yield about twenty-two 1.5-ounce servings when preparing mixed drinks.

❧ A liter of wine or champagne will serve six 5-ounce glasses.

Alcohol comes in a variety of sized containers from 750 ML *(25 oz.)*, 1.75 L *(59 oz.)*, 3 liter *(101 oz.)*, to 4 liter *(135 oz.)*, so adjust your calculations accordingly.

Average Consumption

❧ The average number of drinks per person for a cocktail party is 2.5 drinks.

❧ The average consumption of wine at dinner is two servings per person.

❧ Know your audience. If you know you are entertaining some heavy drinkers, then make the necessary adjustments. Also, if you are entertaining your boss or trying to impress a client, be sure to find out that special brand of liquor he or she prefers.

❧ Do not forget to provide nonalcoholic drinks for your guests. Remember, coffee served after drinking can lead one to feel as though he were sober. Only time, not coffee, can lower your blood alcohol content (which is how sobriety is determined).

Bartenders

If you are having more than twenty-five guests, you might want to consider hiring a bartender. That is, unless you want to stand in the bar all night and mix drinks for your friends.

One bartender can serve up to fifty people, but two are necessary for a group over fifty. If you can set up bars in two different locations, it helps the flow of the party. If you have one hundred guests, three or four bartenders are necessary.

Beer

Beer may be served in the can or bottle at less formal occasions, but should be served in pilsner glasses at a cocktail party or formal occasion. If you are having a large party, you might want to purchase beer by the keg.

Regular keg	15.5 gallons	or about seven cases
Pony keg	7.25 gallons	about 3½ cases
1/6 Barrel	5.1 gallons	about 2¼ cases

If you are buying beer by the keg, you will be required to pay a deposit on both the keg and the tap. This deposit is refundable if you return the keg within the specified time limit. The keg must be kept very cold to maintain the quality of the beer.

Tapping a Keg

Install the tap. Use the pressure release valve to relieve all the pressure from the keg. Then pump once or twice *with the spout open* until beer pours out smoothly. Do not pump any more until the flow of beer lessens. Then make sure you have the spout open when you pump again. Too much pumping just creates foam. I know this will be hard for some men to believe, because they think the harder and more frequently one pumps the keg, the better it is.

Wine

The oldest winery in Texas is the Val Verde Winery in Del Rio, which is over one hundred years old. In the 1970s interest in wine making increased, and now there are about thirty vineyards in Texas. For a population that was better known for washing down Mexican food and barbecue with large volumes of beer, we have come a long way.

Fortunately for the uninitiated, you do not have to be a genius to order wine. Most restaurants have a house wine that the waiter can describe for you. Sometimes restaurants and clubs offer a selection of wine by the glass. Order a glass and see if you like it. A bottle of wine or a carafe usually holds about six glasses of wine.

Matching Food and Wine

The best rule of thumb is the richer the food, the more full-bodied the wine. The old saying red meat with red wine and fish with white wine supports this theory, but if you like a particular wine, it is perfectly correct to order it with any meal you choose. What goes with barbecue? Red Zinfandel or Chianti.

If you are really nervous about ordering wine, visit the restaurant at an off-peak time and talk with the wine waiter or sommelier to get suggestions. You could also ask for a copy of the wine list and take it to your local wine merchant for advice.

The Wine List

The wine list should name the wine, its year, and the producer and price. Wines will usually be grouped by type. Since wine prices tend to be elevated in restaurants, you might want to wait and purchase a very expensive wine at a liquor store and try it at home where it can be leisurely consumed.

The Sommelier

In most restaurants, the waiter will take your wine order and answer questions about the wine menu. In very fine restaurants, the sommelier (pronounced some mill yeah) will take all the wine orders. There is no need to admit ignorance. Just describe what you plan to order for dinner, relate the price range of wine you want, and ask for suggestions. A sommelier's career is based on his or her knowledge of wine. He or she will be very familiar with all the varieties and vintages (years of production) available.

The Server

The server should open the bottle of wine at your table and give the cork to you to look at. If the cork is dry and crumbly or it is wet on both ends, there is a good chance your wine will not taste right. The server will pour a small amount of the wine into a glass for you to taste.

You may have seen people swirl and sniff the wine before they taste it. If the wine smells vinegary, stale, moldy, or like rotten eggs, ask the server to taste it. If the cork looks bad and/or the wine smells bad, you should politely request another bottle of wine. After you have tasted the wine and said it was "okay," the server will then pour wine for your guests.

If you are the guest, allow your host a moment to offer a toast before drinking your wine. (See Toasting.)

Storing and Serving

The optimum storage temperature for all wines is 52 degrees at 60-70 percent humidity. Bottles should be stored on their sides to keep the corks from drying out. White and sparkling wines should be served chilled. Place in refrigerator two hours prior to serving or chill in an ice bath for about 15 minutes. Red wines are served at 65-70 degrees, commonly referred to as room temperature. They are best uncorked a half-hour before consuming to let the full-bodied wine "breathe."

Basic Wine Categories

White (fuller)	*Red (fuller)*	*Sparkling*	*Fortified*
Chardonnay	Cabernet Sauvignon	Champagne	Sherry
	Pinot Noir	Brut	Port
Lighter White	Merlot		
Chenin Blanc	Zinfandel		
Sauvignon Blanc			
Reisling	*Lighter Red*		
Gewurztraminer	Gamay(s)		
	Beaujolais		
Blush (very light)			
White Zinfandel			

Toasting

Toasts may be used as a form of welcoming or congratulating. The first toast should be offered by the host. The guest of honor may respond, and the others may join in. Texans are filled with the spirit of hospitality and relish the moments when they can share special times with good friends. Known for their great one-liners, a Texan's toast can be as entertaining as a good joke.

Rules

- ☙ Never drink when you are the one honored by the toast. Just nod and smile to acknowledge it.
- ☙ Never clink glasses or tap your glass to get everyone's attention.
- ☙ You may toast with any liquid in your glass.
- ☙ Make it short, a minute or less.

How to Toast

Unless it is a casual setting, stand, give your toast, raise your glass while looking at the toastee, drink, and be seated. Set your glass on the table before you sit down.

Composing Your Toast

If you say what is on your mind and do not ramble, you should have a good toast.

> *"I'd like to welcome Helen and Bob Smith to our neighborhood."*

> *"Congratulations to Sara on her promotion."*

> *"Our guest of honor tonight is Elsie Higgins, who is celebrating her 89th birthday. Happy birthday, Grandma."*

Foreign Phrases

> *Skol* or *Salud*, as in to your health
> *A votre sante*, here's to you

Short Poem or Limerick or Saying

"May the road rise to meet you. May the wind be always at your back, the sun shine warm upon your face, and the rain fall soft upon your fields, and until we meet again, may God hold you in the hollow of His hand." —Old Irish saying

Anecdote

Anecdotes can be especially appropriate for a wedding or a roast. Be sure to write out your toast and practice it ahead of time...but no notes, please. These should be no longer than three minutes unless you are the main speaker at a roast.

If you are helplessly unoriginal, there are books with toasts and witty sayings available at bookstores and libraries. Hopefully, the other guests will not use the same book.

Debutante Toasts

The father of the debutante toasts the deb. Her escort usually toasts her, too. The debutante may toast in return, but it is not necessary. Find out what the rest of the group plans to do so you will not be "speechless" if you need to say something.

Father "Karen, your mother and I are so proud of the poised and gracious woman you have become. From the time when you were four years old and wanted to operate on the family dog, you have followed your dream of becoming a veterinarian. Now, only a few years away from your ultimate goal, we just want to say how blessed we are to have such a wonderful daughter. Here's to you on your special evening."

Escort "I have had the pleasure of knowing Karen since we were in preschool. She was a special person even then. She was the only girl we let in our clubhouse. Not only could she field pop flies, but she could catch more fish than any of us. She was, is, and always will be my best friend."

Karen (if she wishes to reply) "Tim, I want to thank you for being my escort, especially when it meant that you had to wear a tuxedo and shave on a regular basis. I could not have a better friend than you. Mom and Dad, anything I have accomplished in life is a reflection of the supportive and caring parents you have been. I love you very much."

Wedding Rehearsal Dinner Toasts

The order of toasts for the rehearsal dinner is the same as for the wedding. The parents of the groom are the hosts at this event, however, and they may choose to start the toasting.

The best man should offer the second toast and serve as master of ceremonies for the rest of the evening.

Wedding Toasts

The best man, as master of ceremonies, should find out ahead of time who wishes to toast so that he can keep things moving in an orderly manner.

Order of Toasts

- best man makes the first toast
- groom toasts the bride
- bride toasts the groom
- father of the bride toasts the couple
- bride toasts the groom's parents
- groom toasts the bride's parents

maid of honor toasts the couple

 mother of the bride toasts the couple

 mother of the groom toasts the couple

 other relatives and friends may follow

Obviously, the parents may combine their toasts, and some steps may be eliminated.

"A drunken tongue tells what's on a sober mind."

Anonymous

Engagements

In days of old when knights were bold...they asked their future father-in-law for permission to marry his daughter. Now, most couples are financially secure, or at least gainfully employed, so the circumstances have changed a bit. My daughter thinks it would be ludicrous for a man to ask her father for her "hand in marriage." What if she did not even want to marry the guy? Okay, propose first, or at least verify the woman is interested. As a matter of courtesy, speak to the prospective in-laws, also.

- When a couple becomes engaged, the groom's parents should call the bride's family. If they do not call immediately, the bride's mom should initiate the call.

- From French terms, the male is referred to as the fiancé and the female is the fiancée. American dictionaries use "feeon say" as the pronunciation for both male and female.

- Engagement rings are not usually engraved.

- Close family or friends may send a small gift to commemorate the engagement. If the gift was not opened in their presence, a thank-you note must be written. (See Wedding Thank-You Notes.)

Formal Announcement

Although seldom seen in recent years, formal engraved engagement announcements may be issued by the bride's parents. These are similar in style to wedding invitations and announcements.

Mr. and Mrs. John William Henry
announce the engagement of their daughter
Karen Melinda
to
Mr. Mark Henry Bower
December the twenty-fourth
Two thousand and twenty-three

Announcement Party

- ❦ You may make a public announcement of your engagement after receiving your ring, usually three to six months before the wedding.
- ❦ The bride's family traditionally hosts the engagement party.
- ❦ The bride's father offers the first toast.
- ❦ An invitation to an engagement party should not mention the fact that it is an engagement party.
- ❦ The groom's family may host a party following this event.
- ❦ No gifts should be taken to an engagement party.

Formal: (if the engagement will be announced at the party)

Mr. and Mrs. John William Henry
request the pleasure of your company
for
cocktails and dinner
Saturday, the thirteenth of January
7 o'clock
1530 Penn Court

R.S.V.P.
732-2609

If the engagement is known, add the lines

honoring
Miss Karen Melinda Henry
and
Mr. Mark Henry Bower

Unlike wedding invitations, the bride's title and surname are used.

Informal:

Ole'! It's a Mexican Buffet
in honor of
Melinda and Mark
Saturday, June 13th
8 o'clock
Cindy and John Henry

Reply   **Casual**
732-2069

A second party given by the groom's family may include the name of the bride-elect, indicating the party is being held to introduce her to a group of people she has never met.

Newspaper Announcements

Your announcement should appear in the newspaper no more than a year, usually three months (but not less than six weeks) before the wedding. Ask if the groom's parents wish to have it appear in their newspaper, too. Check the newspaper's policy on engagement photos/announcements. They can send you a copy of their requirements and any submission forms. In larger cities there is usually a charge for printing announcements.

Materials should be sent to the society desk (or equivalent) at least three weeks before the requested date of publication. Information to include: full maiden name of bride, her parents, the groom and his parents, any grandparents, the date and location of the wedding, and personal history including schooling and jobs. You should include the names of deceased in-laws, deceased spouses, and divorced parents, living or dead.

Be sure to inform your photographer what type of photo you desire. Photos are usually five by seven inches, either black and white or color (no Polaroids). Lightly write your name and phone number on the back side. The traditional engagement photo is only of the prospective bride, but a couple photo is appropriate also. I should not have to tell you this, but leave off the cowboy hats and no romantic poses. Your photo will be available for pick-up at the newspaper office after the announcement appears.

Sample announcement:

> Mr. and Mrs. John William Hunt of Midland, Texas, announce the engagement of their daughter, Delphinium Lynn, to Mr. Archibald Allen Smith, the (or a) son of Mr. and Mrs. Raymond Castor Smith of Middlebury, Vermont. An April wedding is planned.
>
> Miss (or Ms.) Hunt is a graduate of the Boston Art Institute and is employed by Writco

Incorporated. Mr. Smith is a doctoral candidate at the University of Houston.

Broken Engagements

If the engagement is broken, all gifts must be returned with a short note of explanation.

The engagement ring should be returned.

Save the Date

You may inform out-of-town friends and relatives of your impending wedding so that they can make travel arrangements. Do not ask them to "save the date," which implies you expect them to attend. Just let them know when the wedding activities will take place and what hotels they might wish to contact about reservations. Hotels will reserve blocks of rooms, at special rates, for wedding guests.

Gift Registry

Brides have historically registered their china, crystal, and silver patterns at department stores. Discount stores, such as Target, and major hardware chains now provide this service, too. Guests are under no obligation to send a gift from this list, but it can be a very useful shopping aid.

Do not indicate stores where you are registered on any invitation. I do not care how convenient you think it will be for your guests, it is rude. People should call the hostess, the bride's mother, or the store to see where the bride is registered. The only thing worse than putting your registration on an invitation is requesting money, in lieu of gifts, for your honeymoon, house, or furniture purchase. In Texas terms, this is just plain tacky.

Bridal Showers

Bridal showers are supposed to take place after the wedding invitations have been sent but are often held before. You may only invite those people who are included on the wedding invitation list, but all people invited to the wedding do *not* have to be invited to a shower. Guests should not be invited to multiple showers that require gifts.

Do not send party and showers invitations to out-of-town guests who would likely be unable to attend. Members of the bridal party, however, may be invited to all showers and parties. Showers may be hosted by friends of the bride, but not members of the immediate family.

It is proper for the prospective groom to attend any events held for the bride, but it is not required.

Hosting a Bridal Shower

If you wish to host a shower, call the bride or the mother of the bride and specify who the hostesses will be, what type of shower you want to host, and how many guests you can accommodate. Do not offer to host a shower if you cannot attend. The offer of a shower should be accepted or rejected within two days.

If a large number of offers are made, the bride must choose among them. Do not ask the hostess(es) to join with another group of people to have one "big shower." In other words, you either accept the offer of a party as is, or decline it politely.

Hosting a shower does not take the place of giving a wedding gift.

If there are multiple hostesses and /or hosts, they should be listed alphabetically by last name. If the party is being held at a person's home, that person should be listed first. An asterisk is used to indicate to whom to respond on an informal invitation. Include the name for reply on a formal invitation. Remember, never mention where the bride is registered on an invitation.

Shower Invitations

Casual example:

You are invited to a Kitchen Shower
honoring

Suzanne Elizabeth Brown

bride-elect of
Richard Alan Smith

Saturday, March fifteenth
at two o'clock
1604 West Ridge Lane

Kate Stevens*   Sally Hopper   Cindy Ingrid
Sue Jackson   Mary Lemon   Barb Zip

Reply 677-7777*   Casual

Formal example:

> Christina Bates   Rachel Green   Anna Merchant
>
> *request the pleasure of your company*
> *at a Bridal Shower honoring*
>
> **Stephanie Stevenson**
>
> *Saturday, June fifth*
> *at six o'clock*
> *2917 Post Oak Lane*
> *Houston, Texas*
>
> *Please reply (or respond)*
> *Rachel Green*
> *(915) 677-8887*   *Kitchen (type of shower)*

Be sure to include the honoree, date, time, place, the type of shower, hostess(es) name, and response phone number. If a guest fails to respond, it is proper to call them.

The words "bride-elect of so-and-so" may be used on an invitation. It is especially helpful to the recipient of an invitation who is a friend of the groom and may not know the bride's name.

Attending a Bridal Shower

- Respond to the invitation promptly.
- Dress appropriately.
- Call the hostess or bride's mother to see where the bride is registered.
- Take your gift rather than having it delivered unless it is a display shower.

🌰 Shower gifts should be items of lesser value than a wedding gift.

🌰 You do not need to send a gift if you do not attend the shower.

🌰 You may not use your wedding gift as a shower present. Acceptance of a shower invitation requires the purchase of an additional gift.

🌰 Use your engraved calling cards with your full social name for a gift enclosure. Add your familiar name and a note on the back of the calling card. You may also use a plain note card. Include your husband's name only if it is a couples shower.

🌰 Do not ask to bring children or uninvited guests to a shower.

A *display shower* means that the gifts will be delivered unwrapped prior to the shower, and they will be displayed by the hostess(es). A record of each gift should be kept as they arrive. Display duplicate gifts on opposite sides of the room. *Do not* display gift cards, but do tape them to the bottom of the gift or put them inside the box.

Opening the Gifts

If the gifts are to be opened during the shower, each person should be thanked as the gift is opened. Assign someone the task of writing down the gifts and givers for you. If you have thanked each guest personally, you do not need to send a written thank-you, but it is perfectly proper to do so. The hostess should, however, receive a note of thanks and possibly a small gift.

Gift Lists

One of the most important things you need to do is keep an accurate list of the gifts you receive so that you can acknowledge them. Wedding organizers and computer programs specifically for this purpose are available. Find the format you like and keep your list current. If the wedding is canceled, all gifts must be returned to the sender with a short note of explanation.

Other Ways to Help

There are ways to help the bride that would probably mean more to her than another shower. If you are not available to host a shower, or they have already been planned, there are many other things you can do for the bride. You and/or a group of friends can offer to provide any of the following, but be sure to honor the selections of the bride. Do not do anything without first consulting the bride.

- Offer to house out-of-town wedding guests.
- Arrange to take a meal to the bride's house.
- Offer to help the bridesmaids dress for the wedding.
- Take clear drinks and finger sandwiches to the church for the bridal party.
- Help the bride with the church program or any other item that needs to be "assembled."
- Address, seal, or stamp wedding invitations. Offer to go to the post office to have the invitations hand canceled.
- You may "gift" the bride with something she has selected for her wedding: monogrammed napkins, mints, rose petals, or bubbles. Check with the bride or her mother to see where she has selected those items.
- Purchase cake pulls, bride's book, guest book, or cake knife.
- Give the bride a manicure and/or pedicure appointment.
- Compile a handout for the bridal party and relatives listing events, times, directions, pertinent phone numbers, and maps. (See Wedding Schedules.)
- Make welcome baskets for out-of-town guests to be left at their hotel. These can be as elaborate or mundane as you wish: possibly with fruit, crackers, candy, wine, and a map of the city.

Wedding Gifts, or "the Honour of your Presents"

Wedding gifts should be sent to the bride at the address indicated on the back of the wedding invitation. You may enclose one of your calling cards with a message written on the back, signing it informally. If you are a relative, be sure to sign with "Aunt Millie and Uncle Grover" on the back of the card, so that the bride or groom can make the connection. I think that my husband's relatives were unhappy to receive a note addressed to "Mr. and Mrs. _____," but he had tons of relations, and I had only met them briefly. I had a very difficult time putting two sets of names with faces I had barely seen. Of course, that was before men learned how to write thank-you notes.

Remember, you should not take wedding gifts to a shower. A shower requires an additional present. Never take wedding gifts to the rehearsal dinner or the wedding. The family has enough to do without keeping up with gifts, and they may be lost or stolen. You should send a wedding gift within a year of the marriage date. It is acceptable for co-workers or friends to sent a group gift. After the wedding, gifts may be sent to the couple's home.

Checks should be made out to the bride, or to the bride (maiden name) and groom before the wedding, and to the couple following the wedding.

If you receive a gift from someone who is not invited to the wedding, you do not need to invite him or her if you would rather not.

Displaying Gifts

I can hardly write this without smiling. My younger daughter believes that displaying your wedding gifts is a most barbaric custom ... the idea that people would be nosy enough to want to see all your gifts. She just cannot believe it. Many people do enjoy seeing what the bride and groom will start out with, so to display or not depends on the desires of the bride.

Gifts may be displayed at the wedding host's home, usually the bride's mother. Cover tables with white or ecru linens. If rented tables are used, be sure to skirt them.

Checks or money should not be displayed but may be noted on a card without the amount indicated. No gift cards should be displayed with gifts. It is appropriate to set a place setting of china, crystal, and silver and keep the additional place settings boxed. Avoid displaying duplicate gifts.

Check your homeowner's insurance policy for theft coverage while you have so many gifts in your home. Hire a policeman to guard your house during the wedding.

Sip and See

Friends of the bride's mother may host a special day for viewing the gifts at her home, providing light refreshments. A casual invitation with no reply request is appropriate.

You are cordially invited for tea
honoring

Karen Melinda Henry

Saturday, December 7th
at two o'clock
1613 Stanolind Avenue

hosted by
Sarah Crane, Alice Hicks, and Mary Sigler

Wedding Thank-You Notes

Wedding gifts should be acknowledged immediately. All wedding thank-you notes must be sent within three months. (Sorry, but that is the latest deadline I could find in any reference.) After that time, gift givers are well within their rights to call and see if the gift was received. My best tip is try to write most of the notes before the wedding.

I have a friend whose mother wrote all her wedding thank-you notes. Then she sent them, in bulk, to her daughter to mail from her new home. When they arrived, her mother had put the wrong return address on them, so the daughter sent them all back to her. Mom redid the envelopes. I asked her why her mother went to all that trouble. My friend said that her mother just wanted to make sure that her mom's family and friends received nice, well-written notes.

Sent **Prior** *to the Wedding*

The Bride

The bride should use informals, which are white or ecru fold-over notes with her full name or monogram engraved on the front.

Susan Marie Hunter or **S**H**M** or **SMH**

These notes are always handwritten in blue or black ink. The note should begin and end on page three. Do not write on the back of the card.

You may mention the other member of the couple, but you only sign your name. Your return address goes on the back flap of the envelope. It may be blind embossed, printed, or handwritten. It does not include your name.

A certain popular magazine has suggested that the bride and groom combine their initials to form a "couple monogram." There is no such thing! Monogrammed stationery, like your toothbrush, is a personal item and should not be shared. If you wish to have a generic family stationery, it should have no names or initials, but just your address listed at the top of the stationery.

The Groom

The groom should use correspondence cards in white or ecru with a full name or monogram on the top.

David Allen Weidner or **DAW** or **DWA**

Mention the other member of the couple in the note, but only sign your name. The return address is put on the back flap of the envelope. Black or dark blue ink should be used. Just a reminder, thank-you notes are always handwritten.

Content

Be sure to mention the gift and what you plan to do with it. Never mention the amount of a check or cash gift. If you receive a gift card indicating a gift on backorder, you should acknowledge receipt of the card and thank them for the forthcoming gift.

The worst thank-you I ever received, other than a computer generated one, the bride said she was surprised that someone she had not met would send such an expensive gift.

Sent After the Wedding

All of the above applies, except the bride now should use her married social name or monogram on her stationery. Do *not* use Mr. and Mrs. David Allen Weidner (the couples full social names) on thank-you note stationery.

Mrs. David Allen Weidner

or

SWH or **SHW**

Guest List

The bride's parents (or the persons hosting) determine the number of people invited to a wedding. The guest tally can ultimately determine what you will be able to afford to spend on the wedding and the reception. Children of guests (if you wish to include them) can increase the number of guests by twenty-five percent. Reply cards are an extra expense, but if you figure the cost per person for reception food, they actually pay for themselves by allowing a more accurate count for the caterer. (See Reply Cards.) Usually, about one-fourth of the guests will be unable to attend, but you can hardly count on that statistic.

Traditionally, the number of invitations is evenly split between the bride's and groom's family, but there are certainly extenuating circumstances that would make this even division inappropriate. Unless the groom's parents are hosting the wedding and reception, the groom's mother has no say in anything to do with the wedding, except for the rehearsal dinner. She may, however, offer to help with the cost of additional wedding invitations and the resulting increased costs at the reception if she needs to invite more people to the wedding. The ultimate decision on all these matters resides with the bride and groom, and if they choose to have a small or private wedding, their wishes should be respected.

Compiling Your Guest List

You might have already made a tentative list to establish an idea of what your total number of guests will be.

❦ Married couples must be invited as a couple.

❦ Engaged people must both be invited, and so must cohabiting couples.

❦ Unless childrens' names appear on the invitation envelope, they are not invited.

- An invitation should be sent to the clergy performing the ceremony and his/her spouse as well as the groom's parents and the entire bridal party.
- It is proper to include those in mourning on your invitation list.

All names and addresses on formal wedding invitations must follow a prescribed form. Do not submit your list with nicknames or initials. (See Addressing Envelopes for proper form.) Do, however, indicate which guests are relatives, their relationship, and what their familiar names are.

Do not forget ZIP codes. If you do not know them, you can look them up in a book at the post office. Compiling all this information takes a considerable amount of time, so plan ahead.

"If she says, "No," you haven't asked the right question — or the question right."

Anonymous

Wedding Invitations

The most important consideration when selecting your wedding invitation is will it stand the test of time? Select something that will look as elegant on your fiftieth anniversary as it did on your wedding day. Your tastes may change, but good taste never goes out of style.

If you plan to bungee jump, skydive, or marry astride a horse, you do not need to concern yourself with a formal invitation. If you plan something a little more dignified, you will probably want to have a formal wedding invitation.

Paper

One hundred percent cotton paper, sometimes referred to as "rag" (40 pound), is the appropriate paper for formal wedding invitations. It may be white or ecru and have an embossed panel border or a smooth surface.

Ink

Printing

Printing is a flat process where ink is affixed to paper.

Thermography

Thermography is a printing process where a powder is put on top of wet ink and heated to form a raised letter. The ink will be shinier than that used in engraving.

Engraving

A copper plate is etched to make a die for stamping. The paper is pressed into the inked cavity of the die and the ink remains on the raised lettering. Engraving actually makes an indentation in the back side of the paper to raise the lettering.

Black is the appropriate ink color, and all type is centered unless otherwise noted. Invitations may be printed in many script styles, but paneled invitations look better with a tailored script. Leave off the frolicking cupids, entwined monograms, etc. The family crest of the bride may be embossed at the top of the invitation or on the front page of French fold or mock French fold.

Invitation Information

- 🍒 A formal wedding invitation consists of the invitation, the inner envelope, and the outer envelope.

- 🍒 The tissues sent with the invitations may be discarded rather than enclosed with the invitation.

- 🍒 Order your invitations four to six months prior to the wedding.

- 🍒 Order at least two-dozen extra invitations.

- 🍒 Be sure to get a proof of your invitation before they print it. Check everything carefully. A good way to make sure you are actually reading each word is to read it from the bottom up. Have several friends check it, also.

- 🍒 Request your envelopes early. After the return address is embossed, you can send the envelopes to a calligrapher, or start addressing them yourself. (See Return Address and Addressing Invitations for proper form.)

- 🍒 Invitations usually require a fifty percent deposit.

Size

Most invitations are sold with a fold on the left-hand side and do not need to be folded to fit into the envelope. The invitation is printed on the first page. They are usually either 4½" x 6¼" (Crane's Embassy) or 5½" x 7½" (Crane's Royalty).

Traditional invitations are larger and have a second fold. (6⅜" x 8⅞") The fold line runs through the word "to."

French fold invitations begin with a large sheet of paper folded in half, and then in half again, to form a book. The finished size is 4½ x 6¼. The front page may have the bride's family crest embossed on it or may be left blank. The invitation is printed on page three.

Mock French fold invitations begin with a half sheet, folded in half to form a book. The invitation is printed on page three.

Punctuation in Names

🍂 There should be no abbreviations used except Mr. and Mrs., Sr. and Sra. Use full names and no initials.

🍂 Junior and senior should be written preceded by a comma and are not capitalized.

🍂 If you choose to abbreviate them (in the case of an extremely long name), then you capitalize the first letter.

Mr. and Mrs. William Scott Barnes, junior

Mr. and Mrs. William Vandergriff Wadsworth, Jr.

🍂 You do not need a comma before II or III. You may also use 2nd or 3rd rather than Roman numerals.

The Wording

- The word *and* must be spelled out.

- All words should be capitalized except a, the, or, and, etc. and no abbreviations should be used. (Except for junior and senior following a name.)

- *Honour and favour:* The English spelling of these two words is commonly used.

- If the wedding is held in a church, the line reads *"request the honour of your presence."*

- If the wedding is held some place other than a church, the line reads *"requests the pleasure of your company."* This is also used if the reception is held on a day other than the day the wedding takes place.

- *"to"* is used to connect the bride's and groom's names if the invitation is for the actual marriage ceremony; *"and"* is used to link the names if the invitation is for a marriage reception, as in the case of a private wedding. (See invitation samples.)

- *Répondez s'il vous plaît,* abbreviated R.S.V.P. or R.s.v.p., or "The favor of a reply is requested," may be used, followed by the host's address.

    R.s.v.p.
    1302 West Court
    Midland, Texas 79705

- If the wedding is being held at your home, you do not need to include the address in the reply since it will already be in the body of the invitation.

- *Black tie* goes in the lower right-hand corner of the *reception* card if the wedding is formal (It must take place after six in the evening.) It is never put on the invitation.

Arrangement of the Hosts' Names

🌰 If the bride's parents host the wedding, they issue the invitation in their name. The groom's title and surname are used, but the bride's are not.

> *Mr. and Mrs. John William Henry*
> *request the honour of your presence*
> *at the marriage of their daughter*
> *Karen Melinda*
> *to*
> *Mr. Mark Henry Brower (etc.)*

🌰 If the bride and groom issue the invitation, titles are used before their names.

> *The honour of your presence*
> *is requested at the marriage of*
> *(or Ms.) Miss Karen Melinda Henry*
> *to*
> *Mr. Mark Henry Brower (etc.)*

🌰 Use this form if the groom's parents issue the invitation in their name.

> *Mr. and Mrs. William Oliver Brower*
> *request the honor of your presence*
> *at the marriage of*
> *(or Ms.) Miss Karen Melinda Henry*
> *to their son*
> *Mr. Mark Henry Brower (etc.)*

🌰 If the bride's parents are divorced, the proper form is the following.

> *Mrs. Ann Blair Smith*
> *and*
> *Mr. Kevin Alan Smith*

❦ If the bride's parents are divorced and remarried the names are listed like this.

Mrs. Robert Ashton Jones
and
Mr. Kevin Alan Smith

❦ If the stepmother and father have raised the daughter and serve as hosts, their names are written this way.

Mr. and Mrs. Kevin Alan Smith

Titles for Parents on Wedding Invitations

Doctor or Dentist

Doctor and Mrs. Robert Allen Troll

If the female is the doctor, she may use Mr. and Mrs. or

Doctor Sara Troll and Mr. Robert Allen Troll

Judge

If bride's parents:

Judge and Mrs. Robert Allen Troll

If groom's parents:

The Honorable and Mrs. Robert Allen Troll

(Unless they are hosts, then it is Judge.)

President

The President and Mrs. Troll or The President and Mr. Troll

Senator

Senator and Mrs. Troll
or
Mr. and Mrs. Troll

or

Senator and Mr. Troll

Ambassador

The Ambassador of the United States of America and Mr. Troll

Governor

The Governor of Texas and Mr. Troll

State Senate or House

Mr. and Mrs. Troll

Mayor

The Mayor of Midland and Mrs. Troll

Protestant

The Reverend and Mrs. Robert Troll

Jewish

Rabbi and Mrs. Robert Troll

Professional women or women in the clergy usually do not use their titles socially.

The Date

The date should be written in full and may have the word *on* preceding it.

Thursday, the fifth of January (no year)

Time

The time is written out.

at two o'clock
at quarter after two o'clock
at half after two o'clock
at three quarters after two o'clock

If there might be some confusion as to whether it is morning or evening, the appropriate word may be added after the day of the week, or after the time.

Thursday morning, the fifth of January
or
at eight o'clock in the evening

Do not add the word "noon" if the wedding is at twelve o'clock.

Place

Check for proper spelling and wording of the name of the church.

Location

List the city and state where wedding will take place.

Saint Mary's Episcopal Church
Midland, Texas

Receptions

The line

> *and afterward at the reception*
> *Midland Country Club*

may be added with an R.S.V.P. in the lower left-hand corner. Or:

> *Wedding Luncheon*
> *immediately following the ceremony*
>
> *Petroleum Club*
> (add the address if located in a large city)

An invitation with an R.s.v.p. or reply requested indicates that there is a reception and you are invited. A wedding ceremony without reception does not require a reply because by custom, churches are considered a "house of God" and are open to any one. In other words, you are technically replying to the reception, not the wedding, unless it is held outside a church. (See Enclosures for separate cards.)

Sample Invitations

Traditional Wedding Invitation

Mr. and Mrs. John William Henry
request the honour of the presence of

(fill in the full name of guest) line optional

at the marriage of their daughter
Karen Melinda

to

Mr. Mark Henry Bower

Thursday, the fifth of January

at half after two o'clock

Saint Mary's Episcopal Church
Midland, Texas

and afterward at a luncheon
Petroleum Club of Midland

R.s.v.p.
211 North Street
Midland, Texas 79706

Wedding Only Invitation

Mr. and Mrs. John William Henry
request the honour of your presence
at the marriage of their daughter

Karen Melinda
to
Mr. Mark Henry Bower

Thursday, the fifth of January
at half after two o'clock
Saint Mary's Episcopal Church
Midland, Texas

Reception Only Invitation

(In cases where the wedding is private or following an elopement.)

The pleasure of your company
is requested at the wedding reception of

Karen Melinda Henry

and

Mark Henry Bower

on Thursday, the fifth of January
at four o'clock
Midland Country Club

R.S.V.P.
1603 Stanolind
Midland, Texas

Enclosures

Ceremony Cards

(Enclosed with reception invitations when the wedding is private.)

> *The honour of your presence*
> *is requested at the marriage ceremony*
> *at half after two o'clock*
> *Saint Mary's Episcopal Church*
> *Midland, Texas*

Reception Cards

A separate reception card may be enclosed with the wedding invitation when only selected guests are invited to the reception. It should be the same style and quality as the wedding invitation.

Reception
Immediately following the ceremony

Midland Country Club

The favor of a reply is requested
Stanolind Avenue, Midland, Texas

Reserved Seating

Pew Cards

Pew cards might be needed for a large wedding. They are enclosed with the invitation and match the invitation in style and quality.

They let relatives and guests know that a certain seating area has been reserved for them.

> *Please present this card at*
> *Saint Mary's Episcopal Church*
> *Thursday, the fifth of January*

Pew number _____ (bride fills the appropriate number)

Within the Ribbon Cards

These small cards are sent with the invitation, in the same quality and style, and read "*Within the Ribbon.*" They are presented to the ushers to let them know that certain guests should be seated in a cordoned off section of the church. These are usually used for a large wedding.

Reply Cards

Reply cards should not be necessary. All persons invited to a wedding have the obligation to write a handwritten reply to the invitation. Not only do people fail to respond in the correct manner, they do not even return a reply card. If you feel compelled to use a reply card, it should be the same quality and style as the invitation.

> *M*_____
>
> _____ *will attend*
> _____ *will not attend*
>
> *The favour of a reply*
> *is requested before the eighth of December*
>
> or
>
> *M*_____
>
> *will* _____ *attend*
>
> (or no reply date)

If you enclose a reply card, then a response should not be asked for on the lower left-hand corner of the invitation.

Envelopes for reply cards are printed with the address of the persons hosting the wedding and have the postage provided.

Filling in the Response Card

The proper way to fill in a response card is to use the "M" already printed on the card for the first letter of Mr., Mrs., or Ms. and fill in the remaining full name(s) If you have a title other than those, draw a line through the "M" and write the appropriate one, i.e., Doctor.

If you are accepting, write nothing else on the card, if regretting, write "not" in the empty space, or check the appropriate line if given a choice.

Never put the number of persons attending on these lines or reply for individuals who were not listed on your wedding invitation envelope.

Handwritten Replies

Formal invitations always require a formal reply. The wording may sound a bit stilted using third person, but it is the correct way to respond. Use a white or ecru fold-over note and write on the third page using black ink. Send to Mr. and Mrs. John William Henry (your hosts) at the address on the back flap of the invitation envelope.

Normally, you would respond to the hostess only, but wedding responses should be addressed to the couple hosting the wedding. Replies should be made within a week of receiving the invitation. It is perfectly correct to call the hostess and inform her if there is a major problem (family illness or unsettled business) that keeps you from responding immediately.

Acceptance

Mr. and Mrs. Alan Brown
accept with pleasure

> *the kind invitation of*
> *Mr. and Mrs. Green*
> *for*
> *Thursday, the sixth of January*
> *at two o'clock in the afternoon*

Regrets

> *Mr. and Mrs. Alan Brown*
> *regret that they are unable to accept*
> *the very kind invitation of*
> *Mr. and Mrs. Green*
> *for*
> *Thursday, the sixth of January*

- ❧ If your children were invited, their first names should be listed under yours.
- ❧ Do not use abbreviations, and do not put a period at the end of any line.

One or more can go, others cannot:

> *Mr. and Mrs. Alan Brown*
> *accept with pleasure*
> *the kind invitation of*
> *Mr. and Mrs. Green*
> *for*
> *Thursday, the sixth of January*
> *at two o'clock in the afternoon*
> *Samantha, James and William*
> *regret that they are unable to attend*

If a person's name is not listed on the envelope of the invitation, he or she is not invited to the wedding. Never ask to bring dates, houseguests, or uninvited children to a wedding or reception. If you are engaged, then you may ask to bring your fiancé(e). He or she should have been invited in the first place.

Maps

Maps and direction cards may be included with the wedding invitation, provided they are similar in quality and style to the invitation. A mimeographed map really detracts from an engraved invitation. Another option is to have maps available at the hotel(s) where your guests are staying.

Return Address on the Invitation Envelope

The return address, no abbreviations and no names, should be blind embossed on the back flap of the outer envelope. This means the letters are raised, but there is no ink to darken them. The return address can also be engraved, but embossing is preferred. The return address should be for the people hosting the wedding (usually the bride's parents), and replies and wedding gifts should be sent to that address.

Addressing Wedding Invitations

There are two envelopes. The larger is the outer envelope, which has the return address on the back flap, and the front side is used to address the invitation. The slightly smaller inner envelope has the invitees names, only. (See chart.) The outer envelopes are gummed, the inner ones are not.

You must use full names, no initials, and no abbreviations. Lowercase junior and senior should be written out, preceded by a comma, but are not put on the inner envelope. The II and III do not need a comma before them, it is optional.

Mr. and Mrs. and Sr. and Sra. are the only abbreviations allowed: you *must* write out the word "and" between them.

Numbers one through twenty may be written out, or numerals may be used. Street, avenue, city, and state must be written in full.

Calligraphy (a form of hand lettering) is a great complement to wedding invitations. You may choose to hire a calligrapher to address your invitations. Computer generated calligraphy is also available, but a hand addressed envelope is still preferred.

Lines of addressing may be aligned or each line slightly indented from the one above.

Mr. and Mrs. William Henry Bower
1630 Parchment Avenue
Austin, Texas 78705

or

Mr. and Mrs. William Henry Bower
1630 Parchment Avenue
Austin, Texas 78705

Names for Envelopes

Situation	Outer envelope	Inner envelope
Couples living together (do not use "and" to link their names)	Miss or Ms. Linda Williams Mr. Carl Smith	Ms. or Miss Williams Mr. Smith
Married	Mr. and Mrs. Carl James Smith*	Mr. and Mrs. Smith
(if young children invited)	(add)	Thomas and Melissa
Married (wife uses maiden name)	Ms. Cynthia May Jones and Mr. Carl James Smith	Ms. Jones and Mr. Smith

Situation	Outer envelope	Inner envelope
Female	(Ms.) Miss Karen Troll	(Ms.) Miss Troll
More than one female	Misses Karen and Susan Troll	The Misses Troll
Male	Mr. William Robert Troll	Mr. Troll
More than one male	Messers. William and Frank Troll	The Messers. Troll
Very young children (may be included on parents)	The Misses Troll The Master Troll	Marcia Thomas
Ages 6-12 (see parents)	Miss Alicia Troll Gregory Troll	Alicia Gregory

* Children may be included in the invitation to the parents. If you have money to burn, send them their own invitation. Anyone over eighteen should receive a separate invitation.

Do not put "and family" on the invitation. Address it to the parents and include the childrens' names, from oldest to youngest, on the inner envelope under the parents' names.

Single females over eighteen may be addressed as "Miss" or "Ms." Widows use their husband's name. Divorced women may be addressed as Mrs. (Ms.) with her first name (not ex-husband's) and ex-husband's last name.

Mrs. Helen Brown or *Ms. Helen Brown*

"and guest" may be added to the inner envelope of a single male guest and "and escort" (or guest) may be added to the inner envelope of a single female guest. This also will work if you do not know the name or you have not met the other half of a cohabiting or engaged couple.

Relatives

The inner envelopes of close relatives' invitations may use their more familiar names such as Aunt Marie and Uncle John and Grandma, etc.

Unusual forms of address

	Outer envelope	Inner envelope
Doctor – male	Doctor and Mrs. Troll	Doctor and Mrs. Troll
Doctor – female	Doctor Mary Troll and Mr. Mark Troll	Doctor Troll and Mr. Troll
Doctors – couple	The Doctors Troll	The Doctors Troll
Judge – male	The Honorable and Mrs. Troll	Judge and Mrs. Troll
Judge – female	The Honorable Mary Troll and Mr. Mark Troll	Judge Troll and Mr. Troll
Former president	President and Mrs. Mark Troll	President and Mrs. Troll
U.S. Senator	The Honorable and Mrs. Mark Troll	Senator and Mrs. Troll
State Senator or Rep.	The Honorable and Mrs. Mark Troll	Senator and Mrs. Troll or Representative and...
Mayor	The Honorable and Mrs. Mark Troll	Mayor and Mrs. Troll
Ambassador	The Honorable (or Ambassador)	The Honorable and Mrs. Troll
President – male	The President and Mrs. Troll	The President and Mrs. Troll
President – female	The President and Mr. Troll	The President and Mr. Troll

Jewish	Rabbi and Mrs. Troll	Rabbi and Mrs. Troll
(female)	Mr. and Mrs. Robert Troll	Mr. and Mrs. Troll
Protestant		
(male)	The Reverend and Mrs. Troll	The Reverend and Mrs. Troll
(female)	Mr. and Mrs. Robert Troll	Mr. and Mrs. Troll
Catholic	The Reverend Robert Troll	Father Troll

There are books available with endless lists of dignitaries and the proper addresses, including military designations. (See Military.)

Assembling Your Invitation

The invitation is first, the reception card is placed on top, with the reply envelope face down on the reception card and the reply card tucked under the envelope flap. Other items are added from largest to smallest, all face up. If you are using a French fold or mock French fold, the enclosures are placed inside the invitation (which opens like a book) in the same order indicated above.

Invitations and enclosures are inserted into the inner envelope, with the folded edge in first and the engraving facing the back of the envelope so you will see it when you open the envelope.

If you are using a double folding invitation, the enclosure cards go in the same order and are placed at the bottom of the invitation. The top is folded over and the fold goes to the bottom of the envelope.

The *front* of the inside envelope faces the *back* of the outside envelope.

Be sure to weigh your invitations before purchasing your stamps. Additional items or oversized invitations can add significantly to your postage expense. Also, select a pretty stamp and order them in quantity ahead of time. Mail all your invitations on the same day, unless you are sending some overseas and need to allow extra time for delivery.

Wedding invitations should be hand canceled. That means you go to the post office and request that stamps be hand canceled to keep from having large black cancellation marks running across the face of your invitation.

Never hand-deliver wedding invitations.

At Home Cards

At home cards indicate where you will live after you are married. They should be consistent in quality and style with your wedding invitation or announcement.

If included in a wedding invitation, your names are not printed.

At home
after the fourth of August
613 Pinehurst
Dallas, Texas 98021
(972) 934-5600

If they are enclosed with a wedding announcement, the names are included.

Mr. and Mrs. Mark Henry Bower
613 Pinehurst
After the fourth of August *Dallas, Texas 98021*

If you plan to retain your maiden name, indicate the fact on your at home card.

Ms. Karen Melinda Henry and Mr. Mark Henry Bower

At home information may also be included at the back of the wedding program.

Change of address cards of a less formal nature may be sent separately, after the wedding.

Cultural Variations on Wedding Invitations

Catholic Variation

If a Nuptial Mass is being performed, the following additions and changes should be made. (There will be a Communion service if it is a Nuptial Mass.)

> *request the honour of your presence*
> *at the Nuptial Mass uniting their daughter*
> *Karen Melinda*
> *and*
> *Mr. Mark Henry Brower*
> *in the Sacrament of Holy Matrimony*

Deceased parents are listed only on Jewish (with the name followed by a small Star of David) and Hispanic (with name followed by a cross) wedding invitations.

Jewish Weddings

The groom's parents are listed at the top of the invitation, underneath the bride's parents or following the groom's name and "son of."

Hispanic Weddings

Both sets of parents issue the wedding invitation. They may be listed with the bride's parents first, followed by the groom's parents or printed side by side on a folding card.

Carlos Romero Cuevas	*Julio Degas Herrera*
Lucinda Muños de Cuevas	*Manuela Belize de Herrera*
request the honour of your presence	*request the honour of your presence*
at the marriage of their daughter	*at the marriage of*
Sonya	*Sonya Cuevas*
to	*to their son*
Carlos Herrera	*Carlos*

Friday, the sixth of May
at seven o'clock
Saint Anne's Cathedral
Midland, Texas

Bilingual Wedding Invitation

Leonardo Douglas Steed
y
Regina Bendel de Steed
participan a usted el casamiento de su hija
Victoria
con el señor
George Arthur Donnelly IV
que se celebrará en la Estancia Abril
el sábado 13 de diciembre

Buenos Aires, 2010

Transparent overlay in English:

Leonardo Douglas Steed
and
Regina Bendel de Steed
invite you to attend the wedding
of their daughter
Victoria
to
George Arthur Donnelly IV

that will be celebrated at Estancia Abril
Saturday, the thirteenth of December

Buenos Aires, 2010

Kindly reply
Mrs. George Arthur Donnelly III

Enclosure cards for admittance to religious ceremony and reception with Spanish on one side and English on the other.

Lo invitan a la ceremonia religiosa y
recepción que se efectuará a las 19.30

R.S.V.P. 802-3222
804-0666   *Estancia Abril*

You are invited to the religious
ceremony and reception
Seven-thirty in the evening

R.S.V.P. (915) 697-6888   *Estancia Abril*

Enclosure card for admittance to dance, only.

Recibirán a usted después de las 0.30
(Reads, "You will be received after 12:30")

Estancia Abril

Mormon Wedding Invitations

Only members of the Church of Jesus Christ of Latter-day Saints are allowed to enter one of their temples. Invitations are usually issued to the reception. (See Mormon Weddings.)

Mr. and Mrs. John William Henry
request the pleasure of your company
at the marriage reception of their daughter

Karen Melinda

and

Mr. Mark Henry Bower

son of
Mr. and Mrs. William Oliver Bower
following their marriage
in the _____ Temple

Thursday, the fifth of January
from four until seven o'clock

Petroleum Club of Midland

Ceremony cards are included for those guests who are invited to the wedding ceremony. (See Ceremony Cards.)

Wedding Program

While you are shopping for paper products, do not forget the possibility of a wedding program. The quality of the paper used in the program should be in keeping with the style of the wedding invitation. Programs do not need to be engraved. There are many heavy bond papers in ecru or white that would be suitable for this purpose.

The program may be in the form of a small book, usually bound with a ribbon, a fold-over sheet, tri-fold sheet, or just a flat sheet. The cover or heading might contain a cross, both the bride's and groom's monograms, or a Bible verse.

(If you have money to burn, by all means, use rag paper and engraving.)

Items to Include

🌑 Location

🌑 Date

🌑 Couple's name

🌑 Order of worship (include musical selections and responses) The formula is similar to a regular church program.

🌑 Attendants and ushers including hometown and state

🌑 Officials

🌑 Musicians and soloists

🌑 At home notice (See At Home Cards)

Before you discard this idea as another waste of money, remember how helpful it can be to those not familiar with your church ritual.

Wedding Announcements

Wedding announcements are used to inform your friends that you have married. They may be sent if you had a private or small wedding, eloped, or just could not invite all the people you wanted to your wedding. They should be mailed immediately following the wedding. Wedding announcements include the date and *year*. All the same rules apply to wedding announcements and wedding invitations when addressing envelopes.

If the bride's parents announce:

> *Mr. and Mrs. John William Henry*
> *have the honour of announcing*
> *the marriage of*
> *their daughter*
> *Karen Melinda*
> *to*
> *Mr. Mark Henry Bower*
> *Thursday, the fifth of January*
> *Two thousand and ten*

Note the date is written two thousand *and* ten, not two thousand ten.

If the parents jointly announce:

> *Mr. and Mrs. John William Henry*
> *and*
> *Mr. and Mrs. Stephen Allen Bower*
> *have the honour of announcing (or have the honour to announce)*
> *the marriage of their children (or)announce the marriage of*
>
> *Karen Melinda Henry*
> *to*
> *Mark Henry Bower*
>
> *etc.*

If the couple announces:

> *(Miss) Karen Melinda Henry*
> *and*
> *(Mr.) Mark Henry Bower*
>
> *announce their marriage, or have the honour to announce their*
> *marriage, or have the pleasure to announce their marriage*
> *on Thursday, the fifth of January*
> *Two thousand and ten*
> *in Las Vegas, Nevada*

Receipt of a wedding announcement does not require a gift.

Wedding Schedules

It is a very good idea to send all members of the bridal party and the immediate family a list of activities, phone numbers, and a map for the wedding festivities. This may be printed or produced on the computer.

Hotel: London House
    1311 Avenue F
    Austin, Texas 78756
    (412) 363-7755

Bride's Home: Helen and Ralph Bean
    1614 Evans
    Austin, Texas 78751
    (412) 479-0232

Tuxedo Rental:
    House of Coats
    437 Rust
    (412) 363-6678

Rehearsal Dinner: Cole Club
    1602 Bendwood
    699-7909

Wedding: Saint Michael's Catholic Church
    15 Tettleton
    687-0022

Reception: Blaneway Country Club
    311 Overton
    682-7583

Emergency Contact: Susan Hunt 682-7000

❧ List the parties and events, including time, date, location, attire, and who is supposed to attend.

❦ Give specific directions for the rehearsal and the wedding. Indicate what time to be at the church, when photos will be taken, etc.

❦ Enclose a map of the city with pertinent places marked on it.

❦ Set up an emergency contact person who will be available throughout the weekend to take messages or supply help.

"Marry a woman with brains enough for two
and you'll come out even."

Anonymous

The Wedding

There are about 180,000 marriages in Texas each year. With the bridal industry booming and the average cost of a wedding exceeding $18,000, it makes you want to figure out a way to profit from all that connubial bliss.

One of my favorite wedding pictures is of my father, standing in front of a pile of dirty dishes and glasses, with his empty pockets turned inside out, and his hands in the air. He may have tired of footing the bill, but his steady arm was always there to escort each of his four daughters down the aisle.

Wedding Notices for the Newspaper

Notices and a five by seven photo of the bride should be sent to the newspaper at least three weeks in advance. (See Engagement Announcements.) Send all the same information you sent with the engagement announcement, but add when and where the wedding took place, the reception, list members of the bridal party, including ushers, the officiant, and possibly the honeymoon information and where the couple will reside. Remember, large city newspapers charge to print wedding announcements.

I actually saw a wedding photo of the bride and her dogs... no joke. This was in a major metropolitan newspaper. Need I say more? Keep it dignified.

Reserving the Church

Churches fill their schedules rapidly during peak wedding times. Be sure to reserve the church early. Talk with your pastor and confirm that your preliminary plans are in keeping with church policies. Obtain a copy of the church's wedding guidelines. Discuss music and photography. Set your rehearsal time as well.

Also, advise your minister or priest if there will be a large number of guests that might be unfamiliar with church ritual. Ask that he take special consideration to guide your guests through the ceremony. There may be a site fee of $50-$500 and additional fees for the minister and organist.

Civil Ceremonies

Contact the judge or other officiant immediately after setting the date. If you wish to have something other than "by the power vested in me by the state of Texas," you will probably need to develop this yourself. Check the Internet for suggestions on nonreligious services.

The Vows

Do not write your own vows. I have never heard this accomplished successfully. There are books of prewritten vows, but unless you are being married on the beach in a bikini, I would stay away from them. If you want to make an alteration to the vows normally used in your church, talk to your minister in advance. For example, many women do not want the word "obey" in their vows.

Music

Your selection of wedding music will depend on the location of your wedding, but most churches have regulations about what they allow. Save your favorite popular music to be played at the reception. There are numerous tapes and CDs with wedding selections, so you can acquaint yourself with the music before making a choice. Check out the sound system in the church. Be sure there will be someone there during the wedding to handle any sound problems.

Audition soloists, supplemental church instrumentation, and the band for the reception. Ask to listen to demo tapes and check the band's references. They should be able to play a variety of music. Be sure that you request any special music well in advance.

Your contract should specify how many members will perform, what instruments and singers will be provided, when and how long they will play, if they supply recorded music to play during their breaks, and who will be responsible for their meals and lodging. Specify that they pay for any phone calls made from the hotel.

Determine the amount of deposit required and arrange to have someone at the reception pay the band at the end of the party. Also check their cancellation policy. Be sure to tell the band ahead of time how loud you want the music to be. Make sure they are willing to adjust the volume if it seems too loud at the reception.

Musical Selections

The following is a list of musical selections used at the weddings I have attended over the last ten years. Not all music in the prelude or postlude is always identified. Prelude selections start thirty minutes prior to the ceremony. Asterisks indicate the most popular selections.

Prelude:

Trumpet Tune for Beginnings	Baker
God of Grace	Manz
Psalm XIX	Marcello
Jesu, Joy of Man's Desiring*	Bach
Rondeau	Mouret
La Rejouissance	Handel
Andante from Sonata No. 6	Mendelssohn
Praise to the Lord	Bach
Arioso*	Bach
Canon in D*	Pachelbel
Trumpet Voluntary*	Bennett
Prelude in G Minor	Bach
Fanfare from Water Music	Handel
Trumpet Tune	Purcell
Festival Rondo	Purcell
The Heavens Declare	Marcello
Canzana of the Twelfth Night	Gabrieli
Suite from the Cantatas	Bach
Allegretto	Purcell

Seating:

Rondo in G*	Bull
Jesu, Joy of Man's Desiring*	Bach
Trumpet Voluntary*	Clarke
Canon in D	Pachelbel
Greensleeves	Anon.

Processional:

Trumpet Tune*	Purcell
Trumpet Voluntary*	Clarke
Bridal Chorus*	Wagner
Joyful, Joyful We Adore Thee	Beethoven
Jesu, Joy of Man's Desiring	Bach

Recessional:

Hornpipe (Water Music)*	Handel
Allegro - Maestosa*	Handel
Wedding March*	Mendelssohn
Rondeau	Mouret
Trumpet Tune	Purcell
La Rajouissance*	Handel
Hallelujah Chorus	Handel
Musique Royale	Delalande

Postlude:

Toccata Symphony V	Widor
Wedding March	Handel
Final Symphonie I	Vierne

Photography

Select your photographer as carefully as you select your mate. You are counting on the pictures to be a lifetime keepsake of your wedding day. Check out the photographers' samples, get references, and find out who will actually be taking the pictures the day of the wedding. Prices and quality vary greatly. Determine the approximate number of pictures offered with each package and how many proofs there will be. A payment schedule and cancellation policy should be given to you. Your first photo will be the formal wedding portrait, taken before the wedding and used for your wedding announcement. The photographer will usually supply an artificial bouquet to use for this picture, but you may need to make arrangements with your florist for a "picture" bouquet.

Be sure to give the photographer a list of all the *must* have photos: your ninety-five-year-old grandma, your sister's new baby, etc. Assign a friend or family member, without other duties, to point out family members to the photographer. Assess your needs: Do you want lots of posed group pictures or more candids?

Your photographer needs to contact the church and reception site to find out their rules and restrictions on photographs. Most churches do not allow flash photography, and many have restrictions about photos and videotaping during the ceremony.

Find out how long it will be before your proofs are ready and how long it will take to get the actual photographs.

Leaving disposable cameras on the table for guests to take pictures is a nice idea, but I have seen guests take pictures and then take the cameras home, or else they did not take any pictures. Conversely, I have friends who think their guests took better pictures than the photographer. If you plan to use these cameras, request that your guests take pictures, and have a box for them to put the cameras in when they are finished.

Flowers

Obtain references and be sure the florist is familiar with your wedding site. Tell the florist your budget and get an estimate. Make sure the price includes delivery, setup, and any rentals. Items included in your budget would be boutonnieres, corsages, attendants' flowers, bride's flowers, altar flowers, pew decorations, reception decorations, and rehearsal dinner flowers. (See Groom's Expenses to determine his share of the floral purchases.) The bride's bouquet traditionally does not contain colored flowers.

Make financial arrangements with the florist, specifying deposit, when the final payment is due, and their cancellation policy. Remember, you might need a photo bouquet if you are having your wedding portrait taken before the wedding.

The Cake

Bakers will supply samples of their wedding cakes. Select the type of cake, icing, and filling you wish, as well as the design and any accessories. You will probably be quoted a price per person, but you may be able to pay according to the size of the cake. Make sure this includes delivery and setup. Be aware that many reception sites charge a cake cutting fee if they do not provide the cake.

Cake Toppers

The wedding cake is one of the highlights of the reception. No matter what size cake you select, it is like a beautiful piece of sculpture. Do not spoil the effect by sticking a plastic bride and groom or "Precious Moments" figurine on your cake. Cake designers offer many confectionary creations including a variety of flowers and marzipan ribbons. Cakes may also be decorated with fresh flowers or sugared fruit.

Transportation

Transportation for the bride and the bridal party should be arranged for the rehearsal, rehearsal dinner, wedding, and wedding reception as well as any other functions such as a bridal luncheon. This could involve a bus, limousine, or friends acting as chauffeurs.

Wedding Rings

Your wedding rings may be engraved with anything you wish, but the traditional inscription is both sets of initials and the wedding date. The bride should move her engagement ring to her other hand until after the wedding ceremony.

Rehearsal

Churches have wedding directors or volunteers who work with you to explain the rules and traditions of their church. They will attend the rehearsal and walk you through each step of the wedding. They instruct the attendants where to stand and inform them what their duties will be.

Rehearsal Dinner

The rehearsal dinner is hosted by the groom's parents. If they do not live in the town where the wedding is taking place, they may enlist the help of the bride or her parents in locating a suitable site for the dinner. The guest list should include the minister, the soloist and organist (if they are friends), and all those participating in the wedding. Spouses and fiancées should be included. You may also choose to include out-of-town guests.

If the bride's family has an inordinate number of out-of-town guests, they may offer to pay for those meals. Remember, this is the groom's parents' show. While the groom's parents are in charge, they should consult with the bride and groom and try to honor their wishes as to the scale and nature of the dinner.

Invitations

Invitations to a rehearsal dinner should be sent about two weeks before the wedding, but it would be nice to casually inform out-of-town guests if they are invited, so they can make their travel plans accordingly. The time of the dinner should be coordinated with the rehearsal to allow time for overruns at practice and transportation time.

Depending on the nature of the dinner, the invitations may be casual or formal. They should include the name of the honorees, the name of the hosts, the date and time, the place, and city. Be sure to include a reply request so that you can order the appropriate amount of food. Only those named on the envelope of the invitation are invited.

Casual:

Rehearsal Dinner

honoring

Karen and Mark

Wednesday, January 4th
eight o'clock

Carla and Herbert Bower
1611 Hazleton Drive

Reply
672-0146

Formal:

> *Mr. and Mrs. Herbert Allen Bower*
>
> *request the pleasure of your company*
> *at a rehearsal dinner*
> *in honor of*
>
> *Miss Karen Melinda Henry*
> *and*
> *Mr. Mark Henry Bower*
>
> *Wednesday, the fourth of January*
> *at seven o'clock*
>
> *La Scada*
> *Midland, Texas*
>
> *R.S.V.P.*
> *672-0146*

Attire

Since the rehearsal will likely be taking place in a church, dress should be appropriate. If the dinner will be casual, the men can wear khakis, with or without sports coats, and the women may wear casual dresses. If the dinner is formal, men should wear suits and women cocktail dresses. Remember, you will be in church first, so do not wear something too revealing.

Seating

The dinner itself may be held in a home, restaurant, or club and may be a buffet or seated dinner. If there is a head table, the bride and groom, the parents of each, and the best man and maid of honor should be seated there. The father of the bride sits with the mother of the groom, and the mother of the bride sits with the father of the groom. If the rehearsal dinner will be seated, as opposed to a buffet, place cards and a seating arrangement should be used. (See Place Cards.)

For a formal dinner, black ink should be used on the place cards and full names: Mrs. Robert Alexander. (Note: women use their husband's name, even widows, unless they are divorced, then they are Mrs. Elizabeth Alexander.)

Toasting

The host offers the first toast and then the best man acts as emcee. At or before the rehearsal, he should ask who wishes to offer toasts and call on them in an orderly fashion. It is his job to keep things under control and in good taste. Toasts may be offered with any beverage. (See Toasting for other suggestions.) The three most important rules are keep it short, never drink when you are being toasted, and do not clink glasses.

Financial Responsibility

The Groom

The groom pays for the bride's rings, her bouquet, and the corsages for the mothers and grandmothers. He may also give the bride a wedding gift. He is responsible for his tuxedo rental, the minister's fees and license, the rehearsal dinner, and the honeymoon expenses. He also buys small thank-you gifts for the groomsmen and pays for their lodging.

The Bride

The bride pays for the invitations and postage, her wedding attire, floral decorations other than her bouquet and corsages for the mothers and grandmothers, transportation, music, use of facility, the groom's ring and his wedding day gift, and gifts for her attendants as well as their lodging. All reception costs including cakes, food, drinks, rentals, florals, and music are also her responsibility.

Try to use a credit card as frequently as possible, because it allows you some legal recourse if a vendor does not fulfill his contract. Remember that sales tax can add a considerable sum to your bill.

Attire for the Bridal Party

The Wedding Gown

Most brides opt for a traditional wedding gown, but a white suit or dress would also be suitable for a daytime wedding. Wedding gowns are appropriate for widows or divorcees, as long as they feel comfortable wearing one.

Wedding gowns are most often true white or some shade of ecru. Bridal gowns are designed for specific times of the year. Be sure to purchase one that is appropriate to the season during which you will be married. Select your shoes and under garments before you have the dress fitted.

Cleavage. This is the one day in your life where you want to look sweet and innocent or even modest. This is not a time to look like a *Playboy* photo shoot. Cleavage is not appropriate for a church wedding. My mother likes to relate the story my brother told about his elementary school teacher. He said her "lung" fell out of her dress one day at school. You do not want to worry about your "lungs" hanging out of your dress when you are dancing or cutting the cake.

If the bride is wearing gloves (for an evening wedding), she slits the glove on the ring finger rather than removing the gloves. Her gloves stay on except for dining.

The Groom

Depending on the time of day and formality of the wedding, the groom may wear a dark suit or some style of tuxedo. The bride and groom usually make this selection together. The rental store can help you select the proper attire for your wedding. Basically, an informal day or evening wedding requires dark suits with white shirts.

A formal or semiformal evening wedding dictates a black tuxedo, with all the trimmings, and a white tuxedo shirt. White dinner jackets with a cummerbund may be worn in the summer. For a very formal daytime wedding, a cutaway coat is appropriate. White tie and black tailcoat are reserved for very formal evening weddings. Boutonnieres are worn on the left lapel.

The Attendants

Usually the bride and one or more of her attendants select the bridesmaid dresses and headpieces. When selecting a dress, keep in mind the varying weights and heights of your attendants and their coloring. Remember to select appropriate shoes. The bridesmaids are responsible for purchasing their own dress, headpiece, and shoes.

Most stores require a deposit to order the dress and expect to be paid in full before the dress is altered. Allow plenty of time to order dresses and get them fitted. (Sometimes more than one fitting is required.) Also make arrangements to have all the shoes dyed at the same place so the dye lots match.

The Groomsmen, Ushers, Father of the Bride, and Father of the Groom

The rest of the males in the wedding party should wear the same style of clothing as the groom. Be sure to submit all your measurements for a tuxedo well in advance. You need to include your shirt and shoe size. All the tuxedos should be rented from the same place so that they will conform to one style. You may need to provide your own black socks. Each usher and groomsman is responsible for the rental payment on his tuxedo. If you are arriving late or departing early, make arrangements for someone to pick up your rental or return it.

Mothers

The mother of the bride selects her dress before the mother of the groom. The color and style should not conflict with the attendants, but it should not be the same color as the attendants' dresses. An elaborate gown that calls attention to someone other than the bride should be avoided. The mother of the groom may select her dress, keeping the above information in mind. It should be the same length as the mother of the bride's dress.

I have a friend whose son is about to marry, and she told me that she heard that the mother of the groom was supposed to wear beige and keep her mouth shut. She said she liked beige, but the rest might be difficult.

Flower Girls and Ring Bearers

Ring bearers and flower girls are usually ages three to seven. Junior bridesmaids are ages seven to fourteen. Flower girls may wear any color dress that does not clash with the attendants. Ring bearers may wear suits.

Responsibilities of the Bridal Party

Your number one responsibility is to be on time for all functions. Be at the church two hours prior to the wedding (or when indicated) to dress and have photos taken.

Attendants are responsible for their own wedding apparel and accessories. Other costs include transportation, an individual or group gift for the couple, and possibly hosting a shower or luncheon for the bride or a bachelor dinner for the groom.

It is acceptable to have more ushers than bridesmaids, but not the reverse. You may have both a *maid of honor* and a *matron* (married) *of honor*. The maid of honor or matron of honor holds both the bouquet and the groom's ring during the wedding ceremony and adjusts the bride's train and veil, if necessary. (The veil is lifted by the groom or by the father of the bride before he leaves the altar.)

Her duties include collecting money for a gift for the bridal couple and choosing the gift. Remember to keep it in a price range that all the attendants can afford. They will already have incurred many wedding expenses. She may also host a party or shower for the bride (along with the other bridesmaids).

The *best man* arranges for the bachelor party and a gift for the groom, keeping expenses in mind. He also coordinates the pick-up and return of the tuxedos. He delivers the minister's fee, holds the bride's ring during the ceremony, and signs the marriage license. In some cases he will drive the bride and groom to the reception. He offers the first toast at the wedding and is fourth to dance with the bride. He serves as toastmaster at the rehearsal dinner. He makes sure the luggage is in the car and the groom has the tickets for the honeymoon.

Appoint a *head usher* to coordinate and assign jobs. You need to plan on one usher per fifty guests. The ushers should seat all the guests. If there will be an uneven balance of bride's or groom's guests, the ushers should try to fill the pews in a balanced manner. They may tell the guests that they are mixing the bride's and groom's seating.

Females are offered the usher's right arm and are escorted to their seats. (Males walk behind.) If there is more than one female in the group, the eldest is offered the arm and the others may follow behind or wait to be seated individually. A lone male guest is escorted with the usher standing to his left side. (See Recessional.)

Seating the Family

The bride's guests are seated on the left and the groom's guests are seated on the right. (The reverse is true for Jewish weddings.) The bride's and groom's immediate family may be seated ten minutes before the start of the ceremony. They are followed by the groom's grandparents, the bride's grandparents, and the mother of the groom. The mother of the bride is seated, by the head usher or the best man, after all the other guests are seated. After the mothers are seated, no guests should be seated. Any late arriving guests may seat themselves unobtrusively after the entire bridal party is at the altar.

After the father of the bride escorts the bride down the isle and "gives the bride away," he is seated in the left-hand front pew, on the right side of the mother of the bride. During Jewish weddings, both sets of parents stand for the entire service.

If the bride's parents are divorced, the mother sits in the first row on the left with her new spouse (if she has one) and the father sits in the third row on the left, with or without his new spouse. The divorced groom's parents should be seated in the same manner on the right side of the church. Of course, both sets of parents may sit on the front row if desired.

Processional

The minister enters from a side door, as do the groom and best man. The ushers may precede the bridesmaids or may enter at the same time the groom does. The bridesmaids are followed by the maid of honor and the matron of honor, then the ring bearer and the flower girl(s). The father of the bride with the bride on his right arm are last. The mother of the bride should stand when the processional begins. Frequently the minister may also indicate that the congregation should rise. If the church has two aisles, the left is used for the processional and the right for the recessional.

With the exception of the honor attendants, attention should be paid to the heights of the attendants so they enter from shortest to tallest so they look symmetrical while standing at the front of the church. The attendants may be segregated by sex; women by the bride and men by the groom, or they may stand as couples, alternating sides as they approach the altar. Children in the bridal party may stand or be seated for the ceremony.

Recessional

The bride takes the groom's right arm, and the order of departure is reversed for the recessional. Following the ceremony, the father of the bride escorts his wife from the church, following the attendants and officiants. The father of the groom and his wife follow. Single parents or grandparents should be escorted by ushers, and the guests within the family pews should leave before the other guests do.

Wedding Guests

Wedding guests should respond to a wedding invitation within ten days with a handwritten response (see Wedding Responses) or submit the enclosed reply card. (See Filling out the Response Card.) Never ask to bring additional guests unless you are engaged and your fiancé(e) has not been invited. If your name was not listed on the invitation envelope, you are not invited to the wedding and/or reception.

The time indicated on the invitation is the time the wedding is supposed to start. You should plan to arrive twenty to thirty minutes prior to the start of the wedding. Sign the guest book formally, Mr. and Mrs. Herbert Green or Susan and Herbert Green.

The ushers will offer female guests their right arm and escort them to their seat. You may indicate "friend of the bride" or "friend of the groom." If one side of the church is looking empty, you should sit where they seat you. Once seated, guests should not move from their places in the pew to accommodate other guests.

The first four or five rows of pews on either side are reserved for family and special guests. If you receive a "within the ribbon" card in your wedding invitation, be sure to take it to the ceremony. The usher will know to seat you in the designated area. Other times the pews are just marked with special flowers or ribbons to indicate they are for family use. The ushers will know not to seat you in this area unless you indicate that you are a family member.

When you are seated you may greet the people around you, but you should not carry on loud conversations... remember this is church. Unless the church ritual is against your convictions, you should follow along the best you can, but you do not have to kneel. No guests should be seated after the bride's mother is seated. Wait until after the processional and seat yourself quietly in the back. Following the ceremony, allow the immediate family to leave the front pews before exiting.

Never take a gift to the wedding or reception. The only exception to this is certain ethnic weddings where money (in envelopes) is given directly to the bride during the reception.

What to Wear to a Wedding

Black is still a symbol of death and mourning and is not the most appropriate choice for guests to wear to a wedding. I have noticed a growing trend for college age female guests to wear "a little black dress." They certainly do not look as though they were in mourning, but another color would be a better choice. White has long been considered taboo for wedding guests. Avoid cleavage or sequined dresses.

For daytime weddings, the appropriate attire is a church dress or suit. A hat and gloves may be worn. An evening wedding requires dressier church clothing or suits, but no hats.

Men may wear dark business suits day or night. If the wedding is black tie, men wear tuxedos and women may wear short or long cocktail dresses. A dress with a jacket is a good choice because you can be covered up for the ceremony and a little barer for the reception.

Cultural Variations

Mormon Weddings

Only members of the Mormon faith are permitted to attend wedding services at a temple. Children are not allowed to attend weddings held in a temple. Weddings may be held in other locations, however. Guests do not take part in the ceremony, but only observe. A reception may follow the wedding, and gifts may be brought to it. Alcohol will not be served.

Guests at Non-Christian Weddings

Jewish: The wedding takes place under a canopy called a chuppah, symbolizing the creation of a new home. The groom steps on a glass and breaks it during the ceremony, reminding the faithful of the destruction of the temple. The rabbi recites seven traditional blessings. According to Jewish law, a meal must be served following the wedding.

Appropriate attire will vary among different sects, but women should have their arms covered and have their legs covered to below the knee. Men and women may need a head covering. You should arrive at the time stated on the invitation.

Buddhist: Guests will be seated on cushions on the temple floor and should plan to arrive ahead of time. You should not enter the temple during meditation. The ceremony will be brief and possibly followed by a short reception offering light fare, but no alcohol or meat. You should check with your host as to the appropriate attire, but as a rule, clothing will be casual. No gifts.

Hindu: The ceremony has five components: the verbal contract, giving the bride away, welcoming the couple, holding hand ritual, and the seven-step walking ritual. It may take place in a temple or a rented facility. Female guests should not have bare arms or legs exposed above the knee. A reception may be held both before and after the ceremony, but no alcohol will be served. Gifts may be brought to the ceremony.

Islamic: Guest should arrive at the mosque at the time stated. Shoes should be removed before entering the mosque. Women should have their heads, arms, and legs covered to below the knees. The ceremony itself will be brief, usually followed by a reception called a waleemah. There will be food and possibly dancing and music, but no alcohol. Gifts may be taken to the bride's home or to the ceremony.

Receptions

The Receiving Line

Receiving lines are a way to make sure the bride and groom get to greet all their guests. The order should be the bride's mom, groom's mom and dad (if they wish), the father of the bride (if he wishes), the bride, groom, and maid of honor (if she wishes). If the parents are divorced, the parent paying for the wedding heads the receiving line. If they are jointly paying, the bride's mother heads the line.

If the father has remarried and is paying, he and his new wife head the line and the mother of the bride is not in the line. Of course, if the families agree, the bride's mom could be included later in the receiving line. The bride is the only member of the bridal party who may wear gloves in the receiving line, they remain on except while she is eating.

If all this sounds too dreary, remember, you do not have to have a receiving line. Today, guests usually head to the reception while the remainder of the wedding photos are taken at the church. The guests often arrive a good half-hour before the hosts.

Do not stand in a receiving line or go through the line with a drink in your hand.

The First Dance

If the band has been playing and guests are already dancing, the floor should be cleared until the bride has danced with the groom, the two fathers, and the best man. Be sure to consult with the band, disc jockey, or quartet ahead of time and select a piece of music for the "first dance."

The bride and groom start the dancing and the following people cut in.

Bride	Groom
Father	Mother of the bride
Father of the groom	Mother
Best man	Maid of honor

Father of the groom dances with:
    bride, mother of the bride, wife
Father of the bride dances with:
    bride, wife, mother of the groom
Best man dances with:
    maid of honor, bride

Reception Toasts

The bride and groom toast each other before they cut the cake. They may use champagne or a nonalcoholic beverage. At a seated meal, the best man acts as the emcee and the bride's parents offer the first toast. (See Toasting.)

Cutting the Cake

The bride and groom cut the first piece of wedding cake. They place their right hands over each other's and share in the cutting. Traditionally, they serve each other a bite of the cake. This is not a time to ram cake in your new spouse's face. It might get your marriage off to a bad start. I have heard of one wedding where the bride and groom were actually arrested at their reception following a cake fight.

The couple then cuts the first slice of the groom's cake, usually chocolate in Texas. A charming tradition is for each of the bridal attendants to be given a small box with groom's cake to put under their pillow. Supposedly they will dream about the man they will marry.

Tossing the Bouquet

The bride may toss her bouquet to her attendants and other single women, legend being the one who catches it is next to marry. If you wish to keep your bouquet, you may request the florist to make an extra bouquet to throw.

The Garter

I hate this tradition. The idea of the groom removing a garter from the bride's thigh and tossing it to the groomsmen is hardly in keeping with a formal wedding. I have even seen grooms remove the garter with their teeth.

Are You Changing Your Name?

Decide before the wedding what name you will use. Hyphenated last names have dwindled from favor. Options include:

Assuming your husband's name: *Mrs. Robert Allen Cline*

Keeping your maiden name: *Ms. Ann Marie Peters*

Legally changing both names: *Mr. and Mrs. Robert Peters Cline*

You should specify the name you have chosen in the wedding program or on your at home cards.

Report any legal name change to the proper authorities, banks, insurance, government agencies, etc.

The Honeymoon

Make your plans well in advance and purchase cancellation insurance. The year I was married a large hurricane destroyed much of the Gulf Coast and consequently our planned honeymoon.

The License

The state of Texas requires that both parties be at least eighteen years of age. There is a three-day waiting period, and the license is good for thirty days. Minors, age fourteen and over, may marry with their parents' and a judge's consent. Be sure to verify that your officiant has returned the signed license to the license bureau.

Postponing a Wedding

If a wedding must be postponed due to illness or extenuating circumstance, then the families may issue a postponement notice.

Mr. and Mrs. Harold Wendell Harmony
announce that the marriage of their daughter
Jennifer May
to
Mr. Lance Raymond Wilson
has been postponed from
Friday, the fifth of January
until
Saturday, the twenty-first of January
at half after two
Saint Mary's Episcopal Church
Midland, Texas

Postponement announcement with an explanation and no new date:

Due to the sickness (or death) of_____
Mr. and Mrs. Harold Wendell Harmony
announce that the marriage of their daughter

Jennifer May
to
Mr. Lance Raymond Wilson

has been postponed

Canceling a Wedding

If the wedding is canceled due to a change of mind or death in the family, cancellation or recall notices should be sent.

Recall:

Mrs. Harold Wendell Harmony
regrets that the death of Mr. Harmony
obliges her to recall the invitation
to the wedding of her daughter

A new invitation may be issued following the recall of a wedding invitation.

Cancellation:

The marriage of Jennifer May Harmony
to
Lance Raymond Wilson
will not take place
(or)
has been canceled

Mr. and Mrs. Harold Wendell Harmony
announce that the marriage of their daughter
Jennifer May
to
Mr. Lance Raymond Wilson
will not take place

Silver and Gold Wedding Anniversaries

Invitations may be issued by the couple or by their children. They are usually engraved and are similar in style to wedding invitations.

1975-2025

Mr. and Mrs. Arthur John Thompson
Mr. and Mrs. Frederick Emil Thompson
Mr. and Mrs. Rudolph William Muehr
request the pleasure of your company
at a dance to celebrate

the Fiftieth Wedding Anniversary
of
Mr. and Mrs. John Allen Thompson

Friday, the twenty-third of August
at eight o'clock

Burning Timbers Country Club
Plano, Texas

R.S.V.P.
Elaine Thompson
(914) 777-0989

"For better or for worse means for good."

Anonymous

Civic and Charity Events

Texans donate millions to charity every year. We have big hearts and open wallets. Fund raising is a state pastime. With all the worthwhile causes out there, it takes a lot of volunteer workers to raise all that money to do all those good deeds. We are all called upon from time to time (or maybe all the time) to donate our time and energy to some charitable organization.

The first thing you learn is that all of your workers are truly volunteers. You have no control over them. They are there only because they are willing to be there. You cannot threaten them, fire them, or give them a raise. If you are a chairperson, you are at their mercy. Here are some tips to help smooth the path before you.

Chairpersons

I hate to say this, but you need to get a copy of *Robert's Rules of Order.* You may skip to the parts that pertain to your organization, but it is invaluable for settling "discussions." The title is much more odious than the reading. Besides, then you can say, "They are Robert's rules, not mine."

❧ Try to set <u>convenient meeting times</u>.

- Send out reminder cards or call a few days prior to the meeting. (If you have a committee secretary, this job could be assigned to him or her.)
- Always have an agenda and stick to it. Open the meeting, read the minutes, ask for corrections, reports, unfinished business, new business, ask for any further business or announcements, and close the meeting. Then present a guest speaker or program.
- Have hand-outs rather than relying on people taking copious notes. This includes the minutes from the last meeting.
- Define the duties of each subcommittee or officer. This keeps jobs from overlapping and avoids misunderstandings.
- The chair, like the president of a group, should be a facilitator and try to keep the meeting moving, but should not necessarily express their opinions as to the merit of each item.
- Inform all persons who wish to be included in the agenda to call the chairperson at least three days prior to the meeting. Also, they should submit their reports in writing at the meeting. They can read their proposals or report, rather than just rambling. It also gives the chairperson a copy for reference.
- Thank everyone profusely and often. Be sure that all participants are acknowledged at the end of a project. The following excerpt is from a note I received from the chairpersons following the completion of a project.

> *Thank you so much for all you did to make our quilt show a success. What a super job you did in motivating the Wednesday ladies with their raffle ticket sales! Our total sales were wonderful this year.*
>
> *Also, thank you for all the hours you spent working on the day of the show — we were pleased that everything went smoothly. This show definitely takes everyone in the guild contributing to make the show a winner.*

Well, you get the point. They did a good job of letting everyone know that they realized the contribution each person had made to the success of the event. I would work with them on another project, anytime.

The Order of Things

The Proposal

(And I do not mean marriage.) Here is a quick reminder of how the general order goes when you want to bring a proposal before a group.

Member: "I move that we contact the city about our plans to provide $3,000 worth of landscaping for Poplar Park, as designated by the drawing developed by our design team."

Chair responds: "There has been a motion that we contact the city about our plans to provide $3,000 worth of landscaping for Poplar Park, as designated by the drawing developed by our design team. Do I have second?"

Anyone Responds: "I second the motion."

Chair responds: "The motion has been made and seconded that we contact the city about our plans to provide $3,000 worth of landscaping for Poplar Park, as designated by the drawing developed by our design team. Is there any discussion?"

If yes, you may only discuss the motion on the floor, nothing else. After the discussion, then there is a vote. If there is no discussion, then the motion is put to a vote.

Chair responds: "The question is on the motion that we contact the city about our plans to provide $3,000 worth of landscaping for Poplar Park, as designated by the drawing developed by our design team. All in favor of the motion please say "aye;" all opposed say "nay." (Count the votes.) The ayes (or nays) have it."

After the vote, other proposals may be considered.

Members should never interrupt someone when they are speaking. Frame your disagreement in a positive manner: "I disagree," rather than, "that's not right." Speak from a position of strength. Never preface your suggestion with "this may be dumb, but...."

Quorum

A quorum is the number of people that must be present (as stated in the bylaws) in order to conduct business. The quorum of a committee is the majority of its members.

Voting

A <u>voice vote</u> may be used when a majority (more than half) vote is required.

<u>Voting by a show of hands</u> is needed for all motions that require a 2/3 vote to pass.

<u>Ballot voting</u> is used when required by the by-laws or requested by the group.

If there are three or more choices to vote on, the one receiving the greatest number of votes has <u>plurality</u>.

Unless the bylaws of your organization state otherwise, if there is only one candidate for each position and no nominations from the floor, the president may declare the slate <u>elected by acclamation</u>.

Charity Invitations

Being a Sponsor

Your Name

Most invitations to charity benefits list the sponsors' names. When submitting your name with a sponsor pledge, it should be written Sally and Mark Spence (not Mr. and Mrs. Mark Spence). The woman's name goes *first*. If your company has sponsored an event, then submit the company name. You should respond in time to meet the stated print deadline for the invitations.

Seating

If you have a change in plans and are not using your seats or table, call several days in advance so that they can alter the meal count with the caterer. Never move the place cards. The seating at a charity event is determined by the level of sponsorship. If you are not purchasing a table but you want to sit with friends, submit your money and response cards together with a request to be seated at the same table.

Filling Your Table

So you bought a table and now you have to round up three or four more couples to fill the empty seats. Call to invite your guests several weeks in advance. Guests may have to check with a spouse or date before committing, so do not be unhappy if they cannot give you an instant answer. If you have not heard back within two days, you may call and check with them. A week before the event, send a copy of the invitation to your guests. Tell them where and when they are to meet you and what they should wear.

Auctions

Live and silent auctions are popular as fund-raisers. Although you have no legal obligation to remit promptly on a winning bid, you do have a moral obligation to pay for what you bid on. It is a very difficult situation for the charity to be counting on your donation and then feeling uneasy about asking you to make good on your promise. If you are continually waking up Sunday morning wishing you had not bid on anything, switch to ginger ale.

Dress

Most balls or galas will be black tie. Black tie will be printed on the bottom right of the invitation. *Black tie* means a tuxedo for men (the cummerbund goes with the folds up, to catch crumbs) and long or short evening gowns for women. Remember, your diamonds, other than your wedding rings, should not go on until the sun goes down.

White tie indicates that women wear ball gowns and men wear black tailcoats with a white waistcoat and white tie.

Texas tux indicates that the men wear tuxedo shirts and jackets, a cummerbund, and either bow tie or string tie, with blue jeans and boots.

Semiformal or cocktail attire means dark suits for the men and short, after-five dresses for the women.

Casual may mean a lot of different things. I have been caught on this one, so I am extra cautious when I see "casual" on an invitation. The first "casual" party we attended after moving to Midland from Houston, everyone was in sports coats and dressy dresses. The best solution is to ask the hostess what she and her spouse will be wearing.

Dancing

My husband happens to be very willing to dance. He even let me drag him to two sessions of country and western dance lessons. Unfortunately, he is not the typical male. Many men will not set foot on the dance floor.

Most men born before World War II remember the protocol of the good old days...you asked all the women at your table to dance. However, never leave the table to dance if it would leave a woman alone at the table. Men should precede women when walking to the dance floor.

Pictures

Do *not* have your picture taken with a drink in your hand.

Invitations Issued by Organizations

If an organization hosts an event, use a "human" title preceding the organization's name. Examples include The President of, The Board of Directors of, or The staff of.

Multiple Hosts/Hostesses

If a large group of people are hosting an event, there are several ways to list the hosts.

❦ If a group of parents are hosting a party for their children, the invitation may read,

The parents of
(with the children's names listed in alphabetical order)

or substitute "The family of" or "Friends of" in place of "The parents of."

❦ On a fold-over invitation, the invitation may be printed on the first page, with a list of hosts on the third page.

🍃 The hosts may also be listed on an enclosure card rather than on the invitation. The person or couple who are receiving the replies should be listed first, followed by the other hosts listed in alphabetical order.

Endowments

Endowments, scholarships, and donations made be made anonymously or be credited to a group or individuals. If the donation is made by a foundation, then the foundation's name should be used.

The Haverty Foundation
The James Thomas Bell Foundation

If couples or individuals make the donation, the names may be listed in a variety of ways.

Linda A. and Charles P. Smith
Mr. and Mrs. Charles P. Smith

Linda A. Smith, M.D. and
Charles P. Smith

As one fund-raiser commented, "If they are donating the money, we don't care how they want their names indicated."

Junior League

Not having been a member of Junior League, I was amazed at their accomplishments over the past hundred years. I had imagined, stereotypically, it was more like a sorority for grownups. What a wonderful organization and real asset to Texas communities.

History

The Junior League was founded in 1901 by Mary Harriman to involve the community in assisting the disadvantaged. During World War I, the League sold Liberty Bonds and worked in many ways to support America. They helped the suffering population and opened thrift stores during the Depression.

In the 1940s, the Junior League once again turned its attentions to the war effort. The league focused on the problems of education following the Baby Boom of the 1950s. They brought attention to environmental as well as urban issues in the 1960s and also began a drive to diversify their membership in the seventies.

The Junior League is credited with starting the first cancer clinic, starting educational television, supporting legislation dealing with domestic violence, and they are leaders in the field of child welfare. They publish some great cookbooks, too.

Membership

The Junior League's stated purpose is both educational and charitable. There are chapters located throughout Texas. They provide guidance and training for volunteers in the community. Members' job assignments are referred to as their *placement*, and they are required to donate a specified number of work hours each month.

First-year members are called the Provisional Class, or new members. Women are usually recommended for membership and are sponsored by members in good standing, but one may inquire with the local league if she is interested in joining. Women are active members between the ages of eighteen and forty-five, depending upon the chapter, and then they may become sustaining members. Many alumnae go on to serve as leaders in the community and in business.

"What Texans can dream, Texans can do."

George W. Bush

Government

The glittering fact that Texas had its first female governor in 1925, Miriam (Ma) Ferguson, seems quite progressive for a conservative state. Unfortunately, the event was clouded by the fact that her husband and governor, Jim Ferguson, was immersed in scandal and impeached. Jim, driven from office, merely had his wife run in his stead.

Texas boasts two native sons that have served as president of the United States: Dwight David Eisenhower (born in Denison) and Lyndon Baines Johnson, a lifetime Texan. George Herbert Walker Bush, although born in Connecticut, began his oil company in Midland in the 1950s and now resides in Houston. He is rightly considered a Texan, too. Midland's favorite daughter and son, Laura and George W. Bush, have become the fourth Texans to occupy the White House.

Government Invitations

If you are invited to a government function, you should reply to an invitation within a few days of receiving the invitation. Use an engraved (with your social name, *Mrs. Robert Allen Lang*) informal fold-over note in white or ecru. Black or blue ink is proper.

> *Mr. and Mrs. Robert Lang*
> *accept with pleasure*
> *the kind invitation of*
> *Governor and Mrs. Halibut*
> *for Friday, the seventh of April*

If you cannot attend:

> *Mr. and Mrs. Robert Lang*
> *regret that*
> *they will be unable to accept*
> *Governor and Mrs. Halibut's*
> *kind invitation*
> *for Friday, the seventh of April*

If one can go and not the other:

> *Mr. Robert Lang*
> *accepts with pleasure*
> *the kind invitation of*
> *Governor and Mrs. Halibut*
> *for Friday, the seventh of April*
> *Mrs. Lang regrets*
> *she will be unable to attend*

If you would like to add an explanation of your absence, the appropriate phrase may be added after "regret that." Begin with the words "due to" or "because of" one of the following: illness, prior commitment, out of town, or whatever is keeping you from attending.

regret that
due to illness

If you receive a reply card, it should be filled out the following way:

Mr. and Mrs. Robert Lang

_____ will attend

_____ will not attend

Use the "M" already printed as the first letter of Mr., Mrs., or Ms. If you are a doctor or have some other title, draw a line though the "M" and fill in the name(s). Check the appropriate line; never put the number of persons attending on the line.

Contact the governor's office concerning other matters of protocol.

Government Mailing Addresses

The Governor

(To male governor)

The Honorable William R. Halibut
Governor of Texas
State Capitol
Austin, Texas

(To female governor)

The Honorable Winifred Halibut
Governor of Texas
P.O. Box 12428
Austin, Texas 78711-2428

(To male governor and wife)

The Governor and Mrs. Halibut
(home address)

(To female governor and husband)

The Governor and Mr. William Halibut
(home address)

Opening salutation of a letter:

(male)

Dear Governor
(or Governor Halibut)

(female)

Dear Governor
(or Governor Halibut)

Dear Governor and Mrs. Halibut

Dear Governor and Mr. Halibut

Greeting personally:

Governor or Governor Halibut

Mr./Mrs. Halibut

The Texas Legislature

The Texas legislature consists of 32 members of the Senate and 150 members of the House of Representatives.

Senators can be reached at:
The Honorable (Tom Jones)
Texas Senate
P. O. Box 12068
Austin, Texas 78711

Representatives at:
The Honorable (Ann Smith)
House of Representatives
P.O. 2910
Austin, Texas 78768

Letter Salutation:
Dear Senator Jones

Dear Representative Smith

Greeting personally:
Senator Jones

Representative Smith

The Federal Government

Since we have had our share of Texans in Washington, D.C., the following might be useful.

The President   First Lady/First Man   Vice President

Addressing envelopes:
The President   *Mrs. Tuna/Mr. Tuna*   *The Vice*
The White House   *President*
1600 Pennsylvania Avenue   *(no given name used)*
Washington, DC   20500   *Washington, DC*

The salutation:
Dear Mr. President   *Dear Mrs. Tuna/*   *Dear Mr. Vice*
                            Mr. Tuna   *President*

In person:
Mr. President   *Mrs. Tuna/Mr. Tuna*   *Mr. Vice*
                                                        President

Only the presiding president is called "Mr. President." When writing to a former president, the salutation would be "Dear President Chase." When writing about a retired president, he/she may be referred to as former President Chase. The first lady is addressed as Mrs. Tuna. After her term of service, she becomes Mrs. George Tuna.

Letter closings. For the president and cabinet, use *Respectfully yours* for business and *Very respectfully* for social correspondence. For senators and representatives use *Very truly yours* for business and *Sincerely yours* for social correspondence.

The Legislature

Texas has two U.S. senators, who serve six-year terms, and thirty representatives who serve two-year terms.

Senator
The Honorable
(Sandra Benjamin)
U.S. Senate Office Building
Washington, DC 20510

Representative
The Honorable
(Frank Smith)
House of Representatives
Washington, DC 20515

Salutation:
Dear Senator Benjamin

Dear Representative Smith

Greeting personally:
Senator Benjamin

Representative Smith

"A politician ought to be born a foundling
and remain a bachelor."

Lady Bird Johnson

The Military

Texas, being an extremely large state with a considerable amount of political clout, has managed to snare its share of military bases. At this time there are four Army, eight Air Force, four Navy, and one Texas Guard base located in the state.

Military Rankings

Army, Air Force, and Marines
General
Lieutenant General
Major General
Brigadier General
Colonel
Major
Captain
(First) Lieutenant
(Second) Lieutenant
(the Army doesn't use 1st and 2nd)

Navy and Coast Guard
Admiral
Vice Admiral
Rear Admiral
Commodore
Captain
Commander
Lieutenant Commander
Lieutenant
Lieutenant, Junior Grade
Ensign
Chief Warrant Officer
Warrant Officer

Military Weddings

Military weddings are similar to civilian weddings in many ways. If you wish to wed in a military chapel, you must obtain permission from the chaplain's office. Chapels are available on a first-come, first-served basis, and reservations are needed. Neither the organist nor the chaplain is paid for their services, but a donation to the chapel is appropriate.

❧ Your guest list must be submitted to security.

❧ Even if you are planning to marry at a site away from the base, you still must notify your superiors that you intend to wed.

❧ The bride may wear her uniform or a wedding gown, but in either case she may carry a bouquet.

❧ The groom may wear his uniform, but no boutonniere, or he may wear formal wear. Nonmilitary attendants wear tuxedos. All the ushers must wear military dress, or else none of them should. White uniforms are used for summer weddings and blue for winter weddings.

If military parents are issuing the invitation
> *Colonel and Mrs. Robert James Harris*
> (no branch of the service is mentioned)

If the bride is military
> *Captain Linda Patricia Hall*
> *United States Army*

If the groom is military
> *Allen Gale Hill*
> *Ensign, United States Navy*

❧ Navy—Commanders and higher use a title before their name.

❧ Marines—Captains and higher use a title before their name.

- ❦ Army—Captains and higher use a title before their name.
- ❦ Air Force—Captains and higher use a title before their name.
- ❦ The person's branch of service follows on the next line.
- ❦ Junior officers have their title and their branch of service (separated by a comma) on the line after their name.
- ❦ Noncommissioned officers list their branch of service only.
- ❦ The rest of the invitation is the same as for a civilian wedding.

Arch of Swords

The arch of swords is performed by a Naval honor guard consisting of six to eight members. It may be held as the couple leaves the altar or outside, on the church steps, as the couple leaves the church. Only the bride and groom pass under the arch. The ceremony commences at the command "center face" then "draw swords." Then the couple passes under the arch of swords. At the command "return swords," the swords are returned to the scabbards, and with a final "click" (in unison) they are moved the final few inches.

Arch of Sabers

The arch of sabers is performed by an Army or Air Force honor guard. It is held at the end of the wedding ceremony. The commands are "center face" and "arch sabers." The sabers are turned with the blade facing upward, forming an arch. After the bride and groom pass through the arch, the commands are "carry sabers" and "rear face." The honor guard forms the arch again on the church steps.

Saber and sword ceremonies may only be held at the weddings of commissioned service people.

A sword may also be used to cut the first piece of the wedding cake. The groom offers his sword and then places his hand over the bride's to cut the cake.

"Form a battle plan, gather your men and equipment, and attack."

Red Adair

Dangerous Territory

Snakes, Spiders, and Hunters

Texas has four types of poisonous snakes, two poisonous spiders, and over one million licensed hunters. Fortunately, I have not seen any of the snakes or spiders, but I am very familiar with the hunters. "We" own six hunting dogs and an old Bronco that is now worth more than a Lexus. A hunting vehicle is never "done." Ours has been remodeled more frequently than my house. I envision my childrens' inheritance driving across the mesquite disappearing in voluminous clouds of dust.

Hunters

To be specific, bird hunters. I learned to shoot in self-defense. That is, I wanted to spend some time with my husband. Dove season begins about the first of September, and just when I have recovered from that, quail season starts.

My first suggestion is to obtain a copy of the hunting regulations from Texas Parks and Wildlife. Read it. You need to. Courses in hunting safety are taught at many local colleges and are required for hunters born after 1972.

I personally hate to see bird hunters with automatic shotguns because I think having a gun that "breaks" provides more safety when moving around.

If you are leasing hunting property, be sure to respect the owner's land and clean up after yourself. Do not leave shell cases on the ground, and do not shoot toward people, houses, or livestock. Dispose of your mess after cleaning birds. Bird remains attract wild animals that could endanger livestock.

Trees and fence posts that are painted purple indicate posted land. Hunters need to be careful that they remain on their own property or lease.

Dogs have a way of becoming distracted when they are hunting. Be sure your dogs are properly tagged in case *you* become lost. If you have guest dogs, give all the dogs an opportunity to hunt. Train your dog before you go hunting. There is nothing worse than hearing someone continuously cursing at their dog. So, watch your language unless your dog's name really is "Dammit."

Always carry your own kill. If you share your birds with someone else, you need to give *written* permission (your signature and the number of birds) for them to have your birds in their possession. This is very important if a group has been hunting and someone transports all the cleaned birds in one ice chest. Otherwise, you can get in trouble for carrying more than your legal limit of birds. If I sound terribly adamant about this issue, it is because I have several acquaintances who were actually arrested for failure to comply with this law.

Skunks

Nothing can ruin a hunting trip faster than an encounter with a skunk. Although there are a lot of home remedies for removing skunk odor, most of them do no good. The tomato juice version just leaves you with a pink dog.

A more scientific approach was invented by Paul Krebaum, a chemist at Molex Inc. Use one quart of 3% hydrogen peroxide (must be fresh), one teaspoon of liquid soap, and 1/4 cup of baking soda. If you ever made a volcano when you were young, you remember what happens when you mix baking soda and peroxide. Wash your dog with the bubbling mixture and rinse with water. This is enough cleaner for a small dog, but a larger hunting dog or human would require tripling the recipe.

Poisonous Snakes

There are fifteen poisonous snakes in Texas, but they all fall into one of four categories.

Coral Snakes

Coral snakes are red, black, and yellow. Hence the line, "Red and yellow will kill a fellow." These snakes are nonaggressive and reports of bites are rare.

Cotton Mouth

The cotton mouth, sometimes referred to as a water moccasin, is found mostly in wet areas of eastern and central Texas. They have thick bodies and can approach six feet in length. Unlike the coral snake, these snakes are aggressive and will bite swimmers.

Copperheads

Having dark black and brown colored skin, these snakes blend in well with their woodland surroundings and are difficult to spot. They are a menace to campers and hikers. Fortunately, they are the least poisonous of the four snakes.

Rattlesnakes

There are ten different types of rattlesnakes in Texas. The western diamondback ranges in length from three to seven feet and is usually bluish or yellowish gray.

Snakebites

If a snake does not move away when you approach it, back away, moving neither to the left nor right. Almost all snakebites occur around the ankle, so wearing heavy boots is a good deterrent. While snakes do not always inject venom when they bite, poisonous snakes are nothing to mess with. Snakebites begin with a burning sensation that accelerates to severe pain, followed by swelling and restricted circulation.

Treatment

I know you have seen the cut and suck method of treating snakebites in old Westerns, but cutting could actually speed up the spread of venom. There is also a method involving short electrical shocks of DC current applied at intervals to the area around the bite, but most people would not have the equipment or be familiar with how to properly administer this treatment.

The following suggestions are frequently recommended in case of snakebite.

- ☙ Call 911 for emergency instructions.
- ☙ Identify and kill the snake. Take it with you to the hospital or medical facility.
- ☙ Immobilize the victim and provide warmth, if necessary.
- ☙ Use a commercial suction kit to draw out the venom.
- ☙ Clean the area with antiseptic and apply a cold compress.

❦ Immediately transport the victim to a medical facility for treatment with antivenom serum.

Spiders

Black Widow

The black widow spider has a shiny black body with a red marking on its abdomen. While the bite of this spider can make you very ill (stomach disorders, headache, and muscle aches), it is very unlikely to cause death.

Brown Recluse

This is a brown spider with a violin shaped mark on the top of its head and long thin legs.

They range in size from one-fourth to one-half an inch long. The site of a bite will swell, accompanied by chills and fever and a rash, followed several days later by an open wound.

First Aid for Spider Bites

Clean the bite and apply ice. Take the dead spider with you to the doctor for identification.

Scorpions

Scorpions are related to spiders. They have a curved flexible tail, front pincers, and are a yellowish brown color. Their sting is painful but not usually lethal.

Ticks

The large brown ticks that aggravate your dog do not carry Lyme disease. Adult deer ticks that spread Lyme disease are black and red or reddish and are small. Bites cause flu-like symptoms and a circular red rash. Complications can follow if antibiotics are not administered. If you find a suspicious tick, remove the tick and take it to the doctor for analysis.

Use tweezers to remove the tick, grabbing it as close to the skin as possible. Never try to kill a tick while it is attached to your body by using nail polish, petroleum jelly, or burning.

Wear protective light colored clothing when entering wooded areas. Use repellents to discourage ticks. Products containing DEET may be used on the skin but should not be used on the face. Permethrin products will actually kill ticks but should only be used on clothing. When returning from any outdoor adventure, check your body for ticks. It is suggested that you enlist the help of a "friend" to search your body for ticks. Perhaps this sounds like it could turn into something fun, but all I can think of is monkeys picking nits off each other.

"Even a friendly snake is an unwelcome guest."

Anonymous

Let's Call a Spayed a Spayed

I always get a little nervous when the talk turns to animals. Once you get past dogs and cats, my vocabulary declines rapidly. Livestock and related products constitute two-thirds of the annual cash receipts of Texas agriculture, approaching eight billion dollars. It is serious business here. When the topic comes up, do not put your hoof in your mouth.

Pigs

In 1996 Texas produced over 205 million pounds of pork. At the risk of losing all the vegetarians and animal rights activists, when I read that statistic I pictured the world's largest pork tenderloin, gently turning on a spit over glowing coals. Cook mine medium.

Swine – domesticated pig
Pig – swine weighing less than 120 lbs.
Hog – pig weighing over 120 lbs.
Sow – female hog
Javelina – wild pig

Cattle

Texas raises fourteen percent of all the beef cattle in the United States; over fourteen million according to the latest "cow census." Its dairy cows annually produce over six billion pounds of milk.

Cattle – generic term including cows, bulls, and steers

Cow – mature female bovine (usually domesticated)

Calf – young cow

Heifer – young female cow that has not had a calf

Bull – male

Steer – castrated male. This might be the appropriate moment to mention that "Mountain Oysters" are fried bull testicles and yes, they really are served in Texas.

"Braymer" – I had no idea that this was a mangled version of the correct word, Brahman; gray or white cattle with a distinguishing hump on their shoulder.

Santa Gertrudis – the first breed of cattle developed in the United States began in Texas in 1919. It is large, red, and beefy.

Angus – black in color

Brangus – Brahman and Angus cross

Braford – Brahman and Hereford cross

Hereford – white face, red body

Longhorn – descendant of colonial Spanish stock

"Cow chip," "cow pie," or "cow patty" – it's all cow dung!

Beef

The nation's yearly per capita beef consumption is almost 68 pounds. Apart from a few hamburgers, mine is basically filet mignon. Through the years I have eaten many things that have been called "steak," but that have missed the mark. Knowing the lingo is the secret to buying the right beef for the right dish.

What Comes From Where?

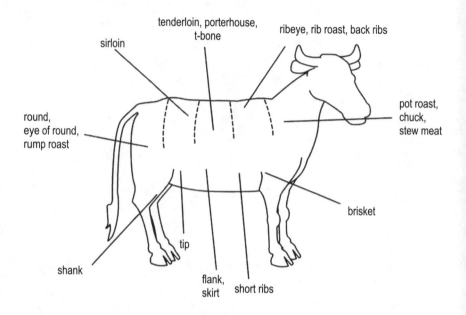

Ratings

Meat is graded Prime (expensive and well marbled), Choice, and Select.

Good enough to stand on their own:

Tenderloin (filet mignon, tournedos, and Chateaubriand)
Rib eye, T-Bone, Porterhouse, and strip (New York or Kansas)
    steaks
Standing rib roast or prime rib

You better marinate and tenderize:

Round steak (as in chicken fried steak: tenderized and deep
    fried in batter and served with cream gravy)
London broil
Eye of the round
Brisket (as in barbecued beef)

Chuck
Flank
Beef ribs

Barbecue

Now that you have read the beef primer, you may proceed to the barbecue pit. Do not confuse the word "barbecue" with throwing some hamburgers on the grill. Barbecue is slow cooked and/or smoked on a grill.

Houston is the home to Jim Goode's retail establishment called the BBQ Hall of Fame, featuring anything related to barbecue. Another Houstonian, David Klose, created a fifty-seven-foot-long smoker capable of feeding 18,000 people. Texans are serious about their barbecue. The sauce wars, spicy versus sweet, rage on, but each chef is convinced his or hers is the best.

Smoking Woods

oak – works well with beef or pork
pecan – fish and poultry
mesquite – (very strong) chicken, beef, or fish

Sheep

Early cattle ranchers resisted the introduction of sheep farming to Texas because they did not want to share their grazing lands. The range wars stopped a long time ago, but sheep farming is on the decline in Texas.

sheep – generic term
ewe – female sheep
ram – male sheep
lamb – young sheep

Goats

There are over one million goats in Texas, and they produce over half of the world's mohair. Although produced mostly for their wool, goat meat (called *cabrito*) is also eaten.

goat – generic term
nanny – female goat
billy – male goat
kid – young goat

Donkeys

I cannot think of anything to say about donkeys; I just loved the idea that the *male* donkey was called a jackass, so I had to include them.

donkey – ass
burro – small donkey
jenny – female donkey
jackass – male donkey
mule – cross of male donkey and a mare
hinny – cross of female donkey and a stallion

Horses

Texans not only raise horses for sale, they use them for transportation and recreation. Many suburban areas have deed restrictions that allow the stabling and pasturing of horses.

foal – young offspring
colt – young male horse
mare – female horse

stallion – male horse
gelding – castrated male horse
mustang – wild Southwestern horse, usually descended from
    Spanish colonial stock
quarter horse – not 1/4 of a horse, but a specialty breed known
    for its ability to run a quarter of a mile faster than any
    other breed of horse

"Approach a mule the way a porcupine makes love;
slowly and carefully."

Anonymous

Funeral Etiquette

Funerals are a part of the grieving process and help a family deal with their loss. Your will should specify the type of ceremony desired and other guidelines so that no one has to make those decisions under duress. Make sure your family knows where your legal papers are located and who the executor of your estate is. I have told my family that I want to be put in a "drawer" so they can move me around to wherever they live. My husband wants to be cremated. . . . I had better die before him because there is no way I am setting him on fire.

Funerals are serious business; that is, it is not the time to conduct business and tell jokes. Speak quietly to family members, relay short anecdotes about the deceased, and offer your sympathies. The best thing you can do for the family is be available to help in the weeks after the funeral. That is the time when the survivors may be feeling lonely, depressed, or overwhelmed.

As time passes, remember to invite widowers and widows to social gatherings. Just because a spouse has died, doesn't mean the other person's social life should come to a halt.

Children

There are many childrens' books that deal with the subject of death. They may help parents discuss death with their child. When the mother of a ten-year-old friend of my daughters died, I noticed that for several weeks both of my children wanted to be where they could see me at all times. I think that when a child is touched by death, they need reassurance that some things in their lives will remain constant.

Whether you should take a child to a funeral is a personal decision. I remember a high school teacher telling me that she was twenty-eight when she attended her first funeral...both her parents were killed in an automobile accident. After hearing that, I have come to believe that it might be a good idea to take a child to a funeral of a distant acquaintance when you feel they are old enough to understand what is occurring. It would give you the opportunity to discuss the funeral and death without so much personal involvement. Parents know their own children's emotional maturity and are the best judges of what is appropriate for them.

Some suggested reading for children and teens:
Lifetimes (Mellonie and Ingpen) any age
A Funeral for Whiskers (Balter & Schanzer) p-3
The Tenth Good Thing About Barney (Viorst) p-3
Nana Upstairs and Nana Downstairs (De Paola)1-3
Emma Says Good-bye (Nystrom) 2-5
I Wish I Could Hold Your Hand (Palmer & Burke) 3-8
The Kids' Book About Death and Dying (Rofes) 6-12

Obituaries

Obituary notices are printed free of charge by most newspapers. Many also allow the option of paying to have a more complete obituary or tribute printed. These should include educational background, the milestones in the deceased's life, military service, employer information, list of survivors, time and place of funeral, and the family's wishes concerning flowers and contributions. Age is not included.

It is not that I do not trust my family to say something better than "she loved to cook and clean house." (I actually read this in an obituary.) I do think, however, that you should indicate ahead of time what you would like in your obituary. If it is going to be the last reminder someone has of you, I would hope it would be a little more indicative of what you have contributed to society. Besides, who really likes to clean house?

It is difficult to believe that any human would stoop so low, but many criminals take advantage of an empty house during the funeral to relieve the already grieving family of their personal property. Either hire a security guard or ask a neighbor to watch your house.

Flowers

The family should designate whether flowers should be sent to the church (some churches have restrictions), the funeral home, the gravesite, or to a residence. The surviving spouse or family orders the flowers for the casket. Friends can send baskets or sprays. Sometimes small floral arrangements sent by children are placed inside the casket. Flowers are not sent to Jewish funerals.

Flowers should be sent either to one of the relatives or addressed, "To the funeral of Mr. Edward Clyde" and sent to the church or funeral home.

Appropriate ways to sign the enclosure card would be,

"With deepest sympathy from the _____ family."
"With sympathy, Robert Smith"

Memorial Donations

If the family members have specified a preference, memorial gifts of any amount may be sent to that (those) institution(s). If the family did not indicate any preference, a gift to any charitable institution that reflects the interests of the deceased would be appropriate.

Condolence Calls

If you are a close friend of the family, a visit to their home would be appropriate. You could also take food, baby-sit, or run errands. This is not the time for long conversations. A short visit and brief expression of sympathy is all that is called for.

Funeral vs. Memorial

A funeral indicates that the body of the deceased is at the site of the funeral service. A memorial service may be held after burial, cremation, or in cases where there is no body.

Cremation

When a body is cremated, the ashes are given to the family. They may choose to scatter the ashes, bury them, or keep them in an urn.

Wake or Viewing

A wake or viewing of the body is held a day prior to the funeral. The casket and flowers will be on display. There is usually a receiving line, and guests sign their names in the guest book.

When Should you Attend a Funeral?

If the funeral is not a private one, you may attend the service for any person with whom you and/or your family has been associated. Funerals are not spectator sports; do not go unless you have some personal or business relationship with the deceased or his family.

You should not attend the graveside service unless you are a relative, close family friend, or have been asked to attend by the deceased's family.

Funeral Dress

Members of the immediate family and pallbearers usually dress in black, with the notable exception of children. Persons attending a funeral are not necessarily restricted to black clothing, but dark clothing in subdued tones would indicate your respect for the deceased and their family.

Pallbearers

If you are asked to be a pallbearer, you will be responsible for carrying the coffin at the funeral and cemetery. Honorary pallbearers do not carry the coffin, but sit in the first pew on the left and leave two by two in front of the coffin. You must serve as a pallbearer if the family requests it, unless there are extenuating circumstances.

If you have ushers as well as pallbearers, the ushers sit in the back of the church. If there are no pallbearers, the ushers sit in the left front of the church. Black or dark suits are appropriate.

The Ceremony

The ceremony will most likely be held in a place of worship or a funeral home. If there is an open casket, you have the option of viewing the body. If you are unfamiliar with the ritual of the church, just follow the standing and seating patterns of the other attendees. Reflect quietly if you are confused as to the oral responses of the congregation. It is okay to talk softly to others before and after the service.

The usual order of entry at a funeral is; the choir, the officiant, honorary pallbearers, the pallbearers and the coffin, the immediate family, others seated in the reserved pews.

Following the funeral, the attendees stand as the procession leaves. The pallbearers and the casket leave first. The casket is immediately transferred to the hearse. The honorary pallbearers exit, followed by the immediate family and guests in reserved seating. Then the other attendees may leave.

A donation may be made by the deceased's family to the church.

Receptions

After a memorial service or funeral, a reception, with or without a receiving line, may be held. This might take place at the church or in a private home.

Signing the Guest Book

There tends to be plenty of confusion at the time of death: out-of-town guests, arrangements to be made, etc. It makes it easier for the family to put names and faces together if you sign with both your first names: Jane and John Smith (ladies first!)

Jewish Funerals

Jewish funerals occur immediately following death. All mourners attend the graveside service. A period of seven days of mourning follows (sitting Shiva) where guests may call on the survivors, but they are usually granted their privacy and the visitors do not converse with them. Flowers are not normally sent to a Jewish funeral, but contributions to charity are acceptable. Food may be taken to the family after the funeral, but it should be in keeping with the family's dietary restrictions.

Guests should wear dark conservative clothing and may be required to wear head coverings, which should be available at the temple or funeral home. If guests participate in the graveside services, they may be asked to put a spade full of soil into the grave. Mourners traditionally wash their hands as they leave the cemetery.

Buddhist Funerals

Family members are not usually visited prior to the funeral, which usually takes place within one week of death. Guest should wear dark clothing and are expected to view the body (there is always an open casket) and give a small bow toward the body. Guests may attend graveside services and visit the family following the funeral.

Hindu Funerals

A Hindu funeral usually takes place within a day of death. The body remains at the family's home, and friends may bring flowers rather than send donations. White clothing is appropriate, with arms and legs covered to below the knees for women. There will be an open casket, and everyone is expected to view it.

Guests may attend the cremation, where a food offering is made and the body cremated. The family may be visited within the first week or so, and fruit is traditionally brought to the home.

Islamic Funerals

Guests at a Muslim funeral should wear dark colors, and women should cover their head, arms, and legs to below the knee. The ceremony takes place two to three days after death and will be held in a funeral home. Flowers may be sent to the funeral, and food may be sent to the family. Guests may attend the interment and may call on the family sometime during the forty days following death.

What to Say

It is sometimes difficult to find the right words at a funeral, but a handshake or a hug and a few words of sympathy go a long way.

If you are attending a funeral:

"My deepest sympathy."

"My sympathy to you...your mother...your family... etc."

"Our thoughts and prayers are with you."

"_____ was a wonderful person and will be missed."

If you are a family member: (in reply)

"Your sympathy is appreciated."

"We will all miss _____."

"I'm glad to meet you, _____ often spoke of you."

"Thank you for coming."

The Funeral Procession

The specified order of the funeral procession will be indicated by the funeral director. In most cases the order is:

- the lead car with the minister and pallbearers
- the body
- the family
- others

If you are driving and a funeral procession approaches, pull to the far right-hand side of the road and stop. Wait until the entire procession has passed before you proceed. Never pass a funeral procession or make a turn through the middle of one. In instances where the funeral procession is on a freeway, those motorists on the access roads do not need to stop unless the procession is exiting in front of them.

246

Flags

A flag should be placed on a coffin with the stars at the head and over the left shoulder. It is not lowered into the ground. A flag flown at half-staff is first raised to the top of the pole and then slowly lowered halfway. Any honorably discharged veteran may receive a flag from the Veteran's Administration at no cost.

Ways to Help the Family

- Organize friends and relatives to send anecdotes, pictures, or favorite memories for a memory book.
- Invite the surviving spouse to dinner, a movie, or play or offer to drive them to church.
- Shop for thank-you stationery, stamps, and a black ink pen.
- Prepare food for out-of-town guests.
- Provide refreshments following the funeral.
- Send short notes or "thinking of you" cards during the following months. Call them frequently.
- Help pack the deceased's clothing.
- Assist with the shopping for funeral clothes or burial clothes.
- Baby-sit small children or the children of visiting relatives.

Sympathy Notes

Even though this is one of the most difficult types of notes to write, it is preferred to sending a card. If you do send a card, be sure to add a personal note on it. It is never too late to send a note of sympathy.

Notes should be brief and end with an offer to help. They should be written on white or ecru stationery with black ink.

Did not know the deceased:

Dear Jane,

> *Bob and I were sorry to hear of*
> *your mother's death. Although we*
> *never met her, we still feel we knew*
> *her in some small measure. Your tales*
> *of her travels were always fascinating.*
> *She will surely be missed by the many*
> *people whose lives she touched.*
>
> *Please let us know what we can do to help you.*
> *Respectfully,*

Friend of deceased:

Dear Carl,

> *Ellen and I worked together on so many benefits, we*
> *became more like sisters than friends. Her greatest wish*
> *was to see the childrens' burn wing at the hospital become*
> *a reality. What a wonderful tribute to her that the build-*
> *ing was completed this fall. Her courage, vitality, and*
> *kindness will be missed by all.*
>
> *We are most anxious to assist you in anyway we can.*
> *With Deepest Sympathy,*

Mass Cards

Members of the Catholic faith may send mass cards announcing that they have requested that a mass be said in honor of the deceased. These should be acknowledged with a thank-you note.

The Survivors

Although there are preprinted acknowledgment cards available, a handwritten note is the most acceptable way to thank those who have served the family. (A flat card or folded note is appropriate.) They might include the clergy, ushers, pallbearers, those who sent flowers or donations or who helped in some way.

The following are parts of two notes I received that I thought were particularly nice.

> *Thank you so much for the note you sent in remembrance of Mother. We were blessed to have her with us for 95 years, but we are painfully aware of her absence at this time. The family and I appreciate your kind thoughts.*

> *With the holidays rapidly approaching, I am more than ever mindful of the blessing I have in the thoughtful friends and neighbors Doug and I enjoyed and shared. I remember the delicious chicken dinner you brought over during those first difficult days after his death. The family enjoyed it so much. Thank you for your notes of encouragement and your caring friendship.*

Responses should be written within six weeks of the funeral.

Widows and Widowers

What should you do with your wedding rings when a spouse dies? It is up to each individual to decide whether to keep wearing the rings or put them away.

Your Name

A widow should be addressed as Mrs. John Smith, not Mrs. Jane Smith, which would indicate she was divorced.

Memorial Stones

Christians usually erect a gravestone within a month of the funeral. It includes the deceased's name, date of birth and date of death, and "wife of" or "mother of" and the survivors' names. Jews erect a memorial stone on the one-year anniversary of the death. There may be a small reception following the event.

Making Your Wishes Known in Advance

While you are still capable of making rational decisions about your own death, it is a good idea to leave a detailed list of your last requests. This should be separate from your will and contain instructions for family members. Address your preference concerning embalming, cremation, or burial, casket and headstone, type of service and music, as well as whether the body should be viewed.

Your choice of burial sites and flowers should also be included. Funeral directors offer pre-need counseling, and burial sites are often purchased in advance. Specifying your desired price range and style of your final arrangements will take a great burden off your family and friends, but remember that inflation may affect your wishes to keep costs to a minimum.

Durable Power of Attorney

Select someone to have durable power of attorney. If you become incapacitated, he or she will handle your money in a way that he or she sees fit. You should use an attorney to execute a durable power of attorney and set any appropriate limitations.

Living Wills

Living wills are a statement about your wishes concerning life-prolonging medical treatment. You may also select someone to have health care power of attorney. This person will represent your medical wishes even if you are not terminally ill but perhaps in a vegetative state. This also should be drawn up by an attorney because the wording of these documents should leave nothing to speculation.

Organ Donation

Texas has a place on your driver's license to indicate that you wish to donate your organs upon death. If you wish to do so or choose to leave your body to science, you need to stipulate this.

Your Will

While it is important to specify your final disposition, having an up-to-date will is also important to ensure that your wishes as to the financial and physical distribution of your property are carried out. I have seen many family arguments erupt over property distribution. Tell each recipient in advance if there are special items you wish them to have. Indicate things of special value such as art, jewelry, or collections that your family may be unaware of. Make sure this is included in your will.

In your will, you name an executor who is charged with carrying out your wishes and filing appropriate tax returns, etc. Your attorney will take you through this process and help you with changes in your will as the need arises. It is important to note the location of insurance policies, bank and savings accounts, investments and mutual funds, and safety deposit box keys. Update this list every year.

The decisions are yours to make, but it makes sense to consult your estate planner or financial advisor, an attorney, and/or your family.

Notifications

When a death occurs the following should be notified:

Attorney, church, funeral home, cemetery, family, newspaper, bank, government agencies, accountant, stockbroker, and executor of the estate.

I had just undergone macular surgery when my father died suddenly. Regretfully, I was unable to attend the funeral. I asked my sisters to relate the details to me. "It was wonderful. The church was filled with all his friends and you could tell just how much they cared for him. The only thing that was wrong was that the flag on his coffin was wrinkled . . . he would have hated that." He was my friend, my kindred spirit, and my remodeling buddy. "Smokey" will be greatly missed by his family and by all the people whose lives he touched.

"The only place some folks make a name for
themselves is on a tombstone."
Anonymous

Index

Look for more books from

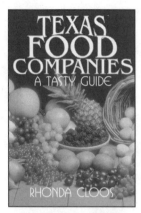

1-55622-877-5 • $18.95

1-55622-886-4 • $18.95

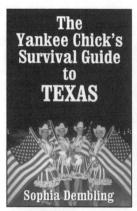

1-55622-888-0 • $18.95

1-55622-827-9 • $18.95

1-55622-641-1 • $16.95

1-55622-569-5 • $18.95

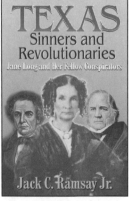

1-55622-835-X • $18.95

1-55622-838-4 • $18.95

1-55622-848-1 • $16.95

For information on our entire list including pricing and availability,

Republic of Texas Press

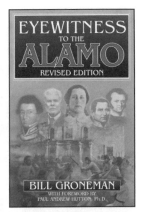

1-55622-846-5 • $18.95

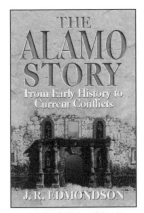

1-55622-678-0 • $24.95

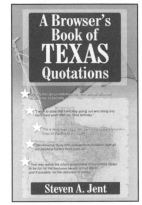

1-55622-844-9 • $18.95

1-55622-786-8 • $21.95

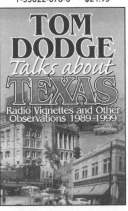

1-55622-779-5 • $17.95

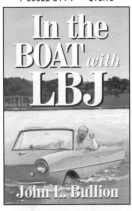

1-55622-880-5 • $21.95

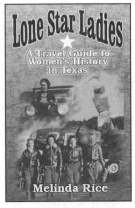

1-55622-847-3 • $18.95

1-55622-624-1 • $18.95

1-55622-796-5 • $17.95

visit us online at www.republicoftexaspress.com.